NOVEMBER 2021

ENHANCING DEMOCRATIC PARTNERSHIP IN THE INDO-PACIFIC REGION

Michael J. Green | Nicholas Szechenyi | Hannah Fodale

A Report of the **CSIS Japan Chair**

ROWMAN &
LITTLEFIELD
Lanham • Boulder • New York • London

ABOUT CSIS

The Center for Strategic and International Studies (CSIS) is a bipartisan, nonprofit policy research organization dedicated to advancing practical ideas to address the world's greatest challenges.

Thomas J. Pritzker was named chairman of the CSIS Board of Trustees in 2015, succeeding former U.S. Senator Sam Nunn (D-GA). Founded in 1962, CSIS is led by John J. Hamre, who has served as president and chief executive officer since 2000.

CSIS's purpose is to define the future of national security. We are guided by a distinct set of values—nonpartisanship, independent thought, innovative thinking, cross-disciplinary scholarship, integrity and professionalism, and talent development. CSIS's values work in concert toward the goal of making real-world impact.

CSIS scholars bring their policy expertise, judgment, and robust networks to their research, analysis, and recommendations. We organize conferences, publish, lecture, and make media appearances that aim to increase the knowledge, awareness, and salience of policy issues with relevant stakeholders and the interested public.

CSIS has impact when our research helps to inform the decisionmaking of key policymakers and the thinking of key influencers. We work toward a vision of a safer and more prosperous world.

CSIS does not take specific policy positions; accordingly, all views expressed herein should be understood to be solely those of the author(s).

© 2021 by the Center for Strategic and International Studies. All rights reserved.

ISBN: 978-1-5381-4047-5 (pb); 978-1-5381-4048-2 (eBook)

Center for Strategic & International Studies
1616 Rhode Island Avenue, NW
Washington, DC 20036
202-887-0200 | www.csis.org

Rowman & Littlefield
4501 Forbes Boulevard
Lanham, MD 20706
301-459-3366 | www.rowman.org

ACKNOWLEDGMENTS

CSIS would like to thank the many experts who contributed their time and expertise in support of this project. Special thanks to Yukio Takasu, Marty Natalegawa, and Dhruva Jaishankar for their insights, which were critical in refining this report. Lastly, the authors would like to thank their CSIS colleagues who contributed research for this report: John Callahan, Jada Fraser, Hannah Goda, Simon Hudes, Seiyeon Ji, Rintaro Nishimura, Kriti Upadhyaya, and Charlotte Voelkel.

The report is made possible in part by a grant from the government of Japan.

CONTENTS

Executive Summary	V
Foreword	VIII
Categorizing Democracy Support Strategies	IX
Funding for Democracy Assistance	X
Case Studies	1
Australia: "Friendly Neighbor"	*2*
Japan: "Good Governance Leader"	*8*
India: "Election Expert"	*16*
Indonesia: "ASEAN Organizer"	*21*
South Korea: "Important Middle Power"	*26*
Taiwan: "Democracy Diplomat"	*31*
Alpha Case: The United States	*35*
About the Authors	37
Annex: A Catalogue of Regional Networks and Institutions	38
Regional Networks	*38*
Regional Institutions	*43*
Global Institutions	*44*
Endnotes	48

EXECUTIVE SUMMARY

In 2019–2020, CSIS began conducting research on strategies for enhancing democratic partnerships between the United States and other regional partners to advance democratic governance and human rights in the Indo-Pacific region. With a grant from the government of Japan, CSIS partnered with the National Endowment for Democracy and the Annenberg Foundation Trust at Sunnylands to research support for advancing democratic norms in the region, hosting a dialogue with leading thinkers on democracy. Based on this dialogue, CSIS published *The Sunnylands Principles on Enhancing Democratic Partnership in the Indo-Pacific Region*, a report containing a set of high-level principles on the role of democratic norms as a foundation for regional stability and prosperity, along with recommendations for policymakers to consider.[1] Building upon this effort, CSIS began exploring new possibilities for cooperation between democratic states in the Indo-Pacific region by researching the various approaches to democracy support among six key U.S. allies and partners: Australia, Japan, India, Indonesia, South Korea, and Taiwan. By characterizing their democracy support activities and identifying common themes, CSIS has identified opportunities for shared efforts with the United States, both bilaterally and multilaterally.

While the United States is certainly a leading player in the Indo-Pacific for democracy support in areas such as human rights, rule of law, women's empowerment, free and fair elections, and civil society, other countries in the region are increasingly contributing to the advancement of democratic principles and norms—often on terms that resonate with their neighbors. Australia, Japan, and South Korea, as Development Assistance Committee (DAC) members of the Organization for Economic Cooperation and Development (OECD), provide official development assistance (ODA) for good governance initiatives and democratic institution building in the region, including support for public administration and legal and judicial development. The Australian government in particular is unique in its ability to support both domestic and regional nongovernmental organizations (NGOs), and Australian, Japanese, and South Korean NGOs all play a valuable role in democracy promotion. In response to rising authoritarianism and democratic backsliding in the region in recent years, all three countries have also begun to emphasize democratic values and support for democracy in their ODA policies and foreign policy strategies.

India, Indonesia, and Taiwan are not as explicit in cataloguing democracy support initiatives, but they do espouse democratic principles broadly defined. India provides technical support and training to developing countries in areas such as support for elections, especially in South Asia. Indonesia, through its Bali Democracy Forum and work promoting democratic values in the Association of Southeast Asian Nations (ASEAN), provides opportunities for countries to discuss important topics related to democracy and human rights. The Taiwan Foundation for Democracy (TFD) supports women's empowerment and the freedom of the press throughout Asia, and a major portion of Taiwan's development assistance goes to providing technical support for Pacific Island countries, which helps to develop civil society in recipient countries. Importantly, India, Indonesia, and Taiwan utilize the power of their example—that is, their own experience with democratic development.

There are also weaknesses in some of these countries' approaches. For example, Japan and India take a "request-based" approach to providing support, which means that assistance must be requested by the government of the recipient country. This approach makes it harder to work with local civil society organizations or to support democracy advocates under autocratic regimes. South Korea has also not prioritized support for civil society groups in deference to the principle of noninterference in internal affairs, though a recent decision to adopt a more grassroots-centered approach to assistance could bolster its democracy-related ODA. India and Indonesia have championed principles of democratic governance, but recent political developments in those countries could affect their efforts to support democracy in the region. The U.S. insurrection of January 2021 that threatened to upend a smooth transition of power could also adversely impact the reputation of the United States in the region. The Biden administration's intention to host a democracy summit affords an opportunity to engage allies and partners on the importance of democratic norms and to identify a range of potential areas for cooperation reflecting the diverse and eclectic nature of democracy in regions such as the Indo-Pacific. Put simply, the United States' strategy for advancing democratic governance in the Indo-Pacific will be more effective if it is made in close consultation with like-minded regional states rather than just delivered from Washington.

CSIS has identified three priorities for U.S. engagement on democracy in the Indo-Pacific region:

- **Engage with Asian Partners during the Democracy Summit's "Year of Action."** As the Biden administration prepares for its virtual Summit for Democracy in December 2021, followed by a year of action and a subsequent in-person summit to review progress in initiatives focused on countering authoritarianism, fighting corruption, and promoting respect for human rights, it should coordinate closely with Asian allies and partners to ensure Asian participation and incorporate regional perspectives. The Indo-Pacific is quickly becoming the most important region for democracy support activities, as it embodies both growing support for democracy and recent evidence of backsliding, such as in Myanmar and Hong Kong, that necessitates coordinated efforts to uphold democratic norms. The United States should work closely with allies and partners to encourage activities reflecting the diversity of regional stakeholders and their experiences with democracy. Encouraging partners in the region to take the lead in dialogue on key issues ranging from women's empowerment to good governance would demonstrate the breadth of support in the region for President Biden's agenda. Where regional allies and partners do take the lead on these issues, there should be opportunities for inclusion of states that might not be attending the democracy summits directly.

- **Utilize the Quad as an Avenue for Democracy Support.** The United States should emphasize cooperation on democracy as a strategic priority for the Quadrilateral Security Dialogue ("the Quad") with Australia, Japan, and India, and it should also network with countries outside the Quad construct, such as South Korea. All these countries are actively supporting democracy in the region but could achieve even greater impact by coordinating their efforts more closely. For example, the United States is working bilaterally with South Korea and trilaterally with South Korea and Japan on women's empowerment initiatives, but efforts should include other partners active in this field, such as Australia, which is especially focused on women's empowerment initiatives in the Pacific Islands. Moreover, these four countries also provide technical assistance, training, and seminars to support legal and judicial reform in developing countries. The United States should therefore leverage the Quad construct to engage like-minded partners and combine resources for initiatives in areas such as women's empowerment and legal and judicial reform.

- **Increase Support for Local Civil Society Groups.** The United States can increase support for civil society groups by assisting countries such as Japan that structure their development assistance around request-based approaches from recipient governments. While these countries may find it challenging to directly fund local civil society groups or dissidents in autocratic countries, the United States has vast experience in this area and could help foster relationships between other donor governments and U.S. NGOs, which have developed networks with local NGOs across the region and can act as a conduit for support. As noted in the *Sunnylands Principles*, supporting democratic development in the Indo-Pacific necessitates a comprehensive approach that involves the diverse actors needed to advance responsive and accountable governance, including civil society, journalists, and governments.

FOREWORD

In 2019–20, with a grant from the government of Japan, CSIS partnered with the National Endowment for Democracy (NED) and the Annenberg Foundation Trust at Sunnylands to conduct research on how to support and advance democratic norms in the Indo-Pacific region. In January 2020, this effort culminated in a dialogue held by CSIS with leading thinkers on democracy to map out strategies for advancing democratic governance in the region. On July 13, 2020, CSIS published a report based on this dialogue, *The Sunnylands Principles on Enhancing Democratic Partnership in the Indo-Pacific Region*.[2] The report contains a set of high-level principles on the role of democratic norms as a foundation for regional stability and prosperity, as well as a background paper examining global trend lines, regional dynamics within the Indo-Pacific, and recommendations for policymakers to consider. CSIS partnered with Freedom House and the McCain Institute in 2021 to produce a more detailed strategy for mainstreaming support for democracy in U.S. foreign policy strategy, culminating in April with the report *Reversing the Tide: Towards a New US Strategy to Support Democracy and Counter Authoritarianism*.[3]

Building upon the central tenets of the *Sunnylands Principles* and the joint project with Freedom House and the McCain Institute, CSIS began exploring new possibilities for operationalizing deeper cooperation among democratic states in the Indo-Pacific region. The strategic assumptions animating this effort are threefold: (1) the success of democratic governance cannot be separated from the goals of achieving a free and open Indo-Pacific order based on rule of law, non-coercion, human rights, women's empowerment, and free and fair elections; (2) there is much broader support for democratic governance in the Indo-Pacific than there is for authoritarian alternatives; and (3) U.S. policies to reinforce open democratic norms in the region will require broader cooperation among democracies and the inclusion of multiple approaches to supporting democratic governance.[4] Put somewhat differently, as the Indo-Pacific moves toward greater multipolarity in terms of power distribution, U.S. policies for democracy support must capture multiple approaches to rulemaking in the region.

In order to set the stage for such an approach and identify opportunities for shared efforts, CSIS has been working with its Sunnylands partners to begin categorizing democracy support activities in the Indo-Pacific region in greater detail. The following report includes case studies on the democracy support efforts of Australia, Japan, India, Indonesia, South Korea, and Taiwan. The report also includes comparisons of democracy support strategies and provides data on democracy-related official development assistance (ODA). Lastly, in addition to the case studies, this report examines how these actors utilize regional networks and institutions to promote democracy support and summarizes current CSIS research on how the United States can partner with countries in the region to advance democracy in these settings.

CATEGORIZING DEMOCRACY SUPPORT STRATEGIES

Figure 1: Characteristics of Government Support for Democracy

Key

Support for democratic institution-building: Clear contributions to various pillars of democracy support, such as good governance, judicial or administrative reform, free and fair elections, free press, and women's empowerment.

Technical support related to development: Technical support for development initiatives related to democracy but not explicitly defined as such. Examples include projects for schools, health, and the development of market economies.

Government request-based: Governments must request assistance from donor countries. Donor countries that use a request-based approach will give "top-down" support only to recipient governments, rather than to civil society organizations (CSOs).

Direct civil society support: Democracy-related support is given not only to recipient governments but also to CSOs operating in recipient countries. Donor countries use a "bottom-up" approach to emphasize public-private partnerships.

Source: Based on authors' research and analysis.

Figure 2: Democracy Support Efforts

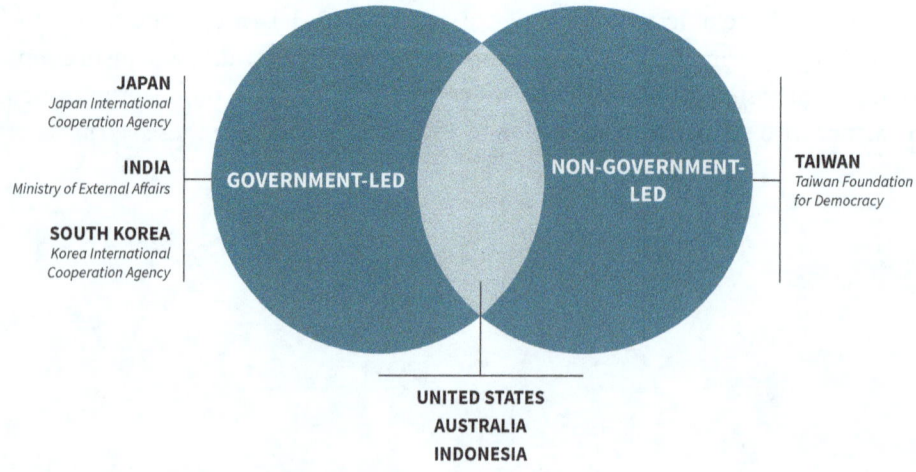

Source: Based on authors' research and analysis.

FUNDING FOR DEMOCRACY ASSISTANCE

Figure 3: Total Democracy Assistance Funding for Asia and Oceania (Government and Civil Society), OECD DAC Countries

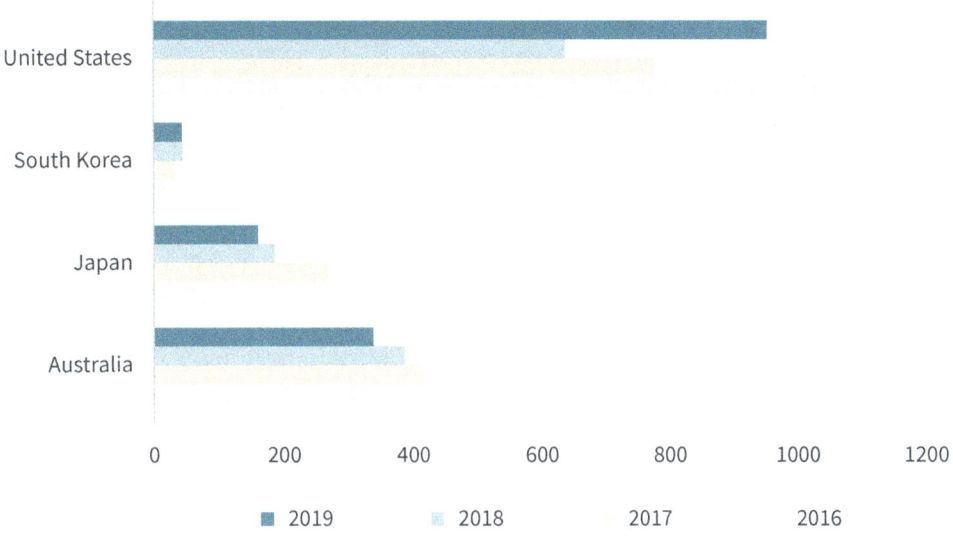

Note: "Democracy assistance" is broadly defined to include ODA related to public administration and management, legal and judicial development, elections, women's empowerment, media and freedom of the press, and human rights. "Asia" includes ODA to Afghanistan, Bangladesh, Bhutan, Cambodia, China, India, Indonesia, Laos, Malaysia, the Maldives, Mongolia, Myanmar, Nepal, Pakistan, the Philippines, Sri Lanka, Thailand, Timor-Leste, Vietnam, Far East Asia regional, South Asia regional, and Asia regional. "Oceania" includes ODA to the Cook Islands, Fiji, Kiribati, the Marshall Islands, Micronesia, Nauru, Niue, Palau, Papua New Guinea, Samoa, the Solomon Islands, Tokelau, Tonga, Tuvalu, Vanuatu, Wallis and Futuna, and Oceania regional. All amounts in USD millions.

Source: "Creditor Reporting System," OECD, https://stats.oecd.org/Index.aspx?DataSetCode=crs1#. Data reflects values for the category "151: I.5.a. Government & Civil Society-general, Total."

Table 1: Highest-Funded Categories and Countries, OECD DAC Countries

Country	Highest-Funded Country (2019)	Highest-Funded Sector (2019)
Australia	Papua New Guinea	15110: Public sector policy and administrative management
Japan	Afghanistan	15130: Legal and judicial development
South Korea	Vietnam	15110: Public sector policy and administrative management
United States	Afghanistan	15110: Public sector policy and administrative management

Source: "Creditor Reporting System," OECD, https://stats.oecd.org/Index.aspx?DataSetCode=crs1#.

CASE STUDIES

AUSTRALIA

"Friendly Neighbor"

OVERVIEW

Australia's ODA is focused primarily on economic development and poverty reduction, with specific aspects of its aid helping to promote democracy. Australia has traditionally placed little emphasis on overt democracy promotion as a foreign policy objective and believes that poverty, rising levels of inequality, and domestic unrest are the root causes of regional instability. Therefore, the emphasis of aid is placed on sustainable economic growth and poverty reduction.[5] However, this has changed in recent years, and the Australian *2017 Foreign Policy White Paper* outlined Australia's commitment to promoting good governance, democratic institutions, women's empowerment, and civil society.[6]

Australia's Department of Foreign Affairs and Trade (DFAT) provides approximately 90 percent of ODA to developing countries. DFAT also works with domestic and international civil society organizations and works to proactively cultivate relationships with local NGOs. For example, projections for Australian global ODA show that AUD 175 million (approximately $132 million) will be allocated to NGOs, volunteers, and community programs, and AUD 420 million (approximately $316 million) will be allocated to Indo-Pacific sectoral programs.[7] Australia also provides ample opportunities for the private sector to participate in development activities.

Specific to democracy support, Australian ODA is heavily focused on women's empowerment. In 2019, Australia committed 37.9 percent of its screened bilateral allocable aid to gender equality and women's empowerment overall, though this was down from 44 percent in 2018.[8] Australia is also the largest donor in the Pacific Islands region, with a 60 percent share of total OECD aid to the Pacific Islands.[9] The Pacific region is projected to receive AUD 1.44 billion (approximately $1.08 billion) in 2020–21, the largest share of Australian ODA globally.[10]

BACKGROUND AND RECENT TRENDS

Though Australia's ODA strategy has not traditionally emphasized democracy promotion, recent regional developments have caused Australia to focus more of its efforts on democracy support. Australia's *2017 Foreign Policy White Paper* identified rising authoritarianism in the region as a challenge to Australia's security interests and highlighted Australia's normative commitment to democracy promotion: "It is strongly in Australia's interests to seek to prevent the erosion of hard-won international rules and agreed norms of behaviour that promote global security."[11] It outlines Australia's commitment to promoting and strengthening good governance, democratic institutions, women's empowerment, and civil society, while also outlining the shift in Australian ODA toward the Indo-Pacific region.[12] It states that China's power and influence in the region is particularly worrying and that the future balance of power will largely depend on the actions of major powers in the region.[13]

While Australia's ODA policy may be impacted by strategic considerations, stakeholders have pointed out that Australia describes its aid in instrumentalist terms as a tool for extending Australian interests in the region or in terms of Australian generosity in providing charity.[14] This is because the political class has historically seen aid as "charity" and not a foreign policy tool.[15] Despite 17 of Australia's closest 20 neighbors being aid recipients, Australia's aid program has been cut by almost a third from its AUD 5.5 billion (approximately $4.14 billion) peak in 2013–2014.[16] When measured as a portion of Australia's gross national income, the ODA budget is now at its least generous levels in history.[17] Based on OECD data between 2010 and 2019, Australian aid in the "government and civil society general" category—most directly related to democracy promotion—has increased in South and Central Asia by approximately 56 percent, decreased in East Asia by approximately 36 percent, and decreased in the Pacific region by approximately 42 percent.[18]

DFAT prefers to invest in the skills of generalists and outsource implementation of projects to contractors, the majority of which are private contractors and multilateral organizations.[19] Therefore, DFAT funds many of its democracy support initiatives through nonprofit organizations, such as the Asia Foundation. Australia has experience implementing public-private partnerships, working with NGOs, and collaborating bilaterally with other countries (e.g., New Zealand). Australia's contributions to multilateral organizations are mainly allocated to the United Nations, the World Bank Group, and regional development banks.[20]

GOVERNMENT SUPPORT FOR DEMOCRACY-RELATED INITIATIVES

Good Governance

Australia identifies ineffective governance as the core issue with most development challenges in recipient countries. This takes many forms, from poor policy decisions to ineffective judicial systems and disorganized bureaucracies. DFAT also provides institutional support to promote sustainable economic growth and poverty reduction, based on the premise that generating growth requires an appropriate policy and regulatory framework as well as effective institutions to facilitate implementation. Highlights are as follows:

- DFAT funds global, regional, and bilateral governance, along with anti-corruption and justice programs that primarily focus on governance issues. An estimated AUD 743.1 million (approximately $559.5 million) was allocated to governance in 2020–21.[21]

- The Development Leadership Program (DLP) is an "international research-led policy initiative that explores the critical role that leaders and leadership coalitions play in promoting or hindering development outcomes."[22] A total of AUD 2.7 million (approximately $2 million) has been committed between January 2018 and June 2022. The DLP focuses on "the role of homegrown leadership and coalitions in forging legitimate institutions that promote sustainable growth, political stability, and inclusive social development," as well as on the role internal and external actors play in supporting these institutions.[23]

- The Indo-Pacific Partnerships Program is managed by Transparency International, a German NGO. It combats corruption and helps communities in 10 countries strengthen transparency, accountability, and integrity. A total of AUD 9.25 million (approximately $6.96 million) was committed by DFAT and New Zealand's Ministry of Foreign Affairs and Trade between January 2020 and February 2024.[24]

- The Australian Department of Home Affairs' Indo-Pacific Justice and Security Program (IP-JuSP) assists partner countries to strengthen their legal, policy, and institutional responses to transnational crime and violent extremism.[25] DFAT has committed

AUD 15.8 million (approximately $11.9 million) to this program between July 2017 and June 2021. The Department of Home Affairs manages implementation, drawing on technical expertise and peer-to-peer credibility of officers from the Department of Home Affairs, the Attorney-General's Department, and the Australian Border Force. IP-JuSP focuses on engaging with developing countries in South and Southeast Asia to enhance their legal and policy responses to financial crime and illicit financial flows, exploitative irregular migration, and international crime cooperation. IP-JuSP responds to requests from partner countries.[26]

Women's Empowerment and Gender Equality

Australia supports various activities to enhance women's economic empowerment. Examples include:

- The Gender Equality Fund is one of Australia's largest programs dedicated to women's empowerment. The fund was established in 2015 to strengthen work on gender equality and women's empowerment in Australia's ODA. A total of AUD 75 million (approximately $56 million) was provided for 2020–21.[27]

- The Investing in Women program aims to improve women's economic participation as employees and as entrepreneurs and influence the private and public sector environment to promote empowerment in Southeast Asia. A total of AUD 102 million (approximately $77 million) has been provided to Indonesia, Vietnam, the Philippines, and Myanmar between 2016 and 2023.[28]

- The Pacific Women Shaping Pacific Development (Pacific Women) program was established in 2012 and has supported more than 160 partners across 14 Pacific Island countries to increase the safety of Pacific women and girls and improve their political, economic, and social opportunities.[29] The initiative is funded from 2012 through 2022, with a total of AUD 320 million (approximately $241 million). Activities include the Pacific Women's Parliamentary Partnership Project, which helps build the capacity of Pacific women members of parliament and staff, as well as the institutions in which they work, to better address gender inequalities in Pacific parliaments.[30] In addition, Pacific Women provides support for research at academic institutions into the factors that allow for women's success in political leadership. One example is the State, Society and Governance in Melanesia Program's report, *Women's Political and Administrative Leadership in the Pacific*, published by the Australian National University.[31] Lastly, Pacific Women provides support for Pacific Island governments to integrate gender equality and women's empowerment into their policies, legislation, and programs. Pacific Women will be replaced by Pacific Women Lead, which will focus on "women's leadership, women's rights, and increasing the effectiveness of regional gender equality efforts."[32] AUD 170 million (approximately $128 million) has been allocated for this program between 2021 and 2026, with the potential for an extension to 2029.[33]

Capacity Building

In Australia's neighborhood, 15 of its nearest neighbors are among the world's least-developed countries, and 7 of the top 10 recipients of Australian ODA are regarded as "fragile." DFAT, therefore, considers promotion of stability through capacity building initiatives as an Australian national interest. Specifically, Australia provides support to countries either "emerging from or at risk of descending into violent conflict." It works with a range of local and international partners to "prevent or reduce violence, protect people and key institutions, and promote political processes which are conducted without resort to armed violence." This includes efforts to "generate employment and livelihoods, ensure the delivery of basic services, and build core capacity to manage political, security, and development processes."[34]

- The Justice Services Stability for Development program in Papua New Guinea is an example of institutional capacity building in law and justice. Phase one of the program ran from January 2016 through December 2020, and phase two of the program commenced in January 2021 and will run until December 2023. The program aims to strengthen the capacity of Papua New Guinea's law and justice agencies to deliver services in a variety of areas related to the judicial and legal system. These include crime prevention, policing, persecutions, legal aid, and prisons. Phase two of the program specifically focuses on the development and implementation of inclusive legal and policy initiatives and services, including for women and children. In phase two, DFAT will also coordinate local delivery of justice services and improve accessibility and enforcement in priority areas such as anti-corruption and juvenile justice.[35]

- The Australian NGO Cooperation Program (ANCP) aims to build the capacity of in-country implementing partners and communities. The ANCP is integral in partnering Australian-based international development NGOs with DFAT, and it supports governance, capacity building (including strengthening the organizational, planning, management, and accountability capacities of local NGOs), and the overall strengthening of civil society through its work with Australian NGOs.[36]

- The Strategic Partnership on Sub-national Governance Program was funded by DFAT and implemented by the Asia Foundation. It used capacity building in governance to help subnational Nepalese governments become stronger, more effective, and more inclusive.[37] The program started in February 2017 and ran until April 2021, with a budget of AUD 20 million (approximately $15 million). Its priorities consisted of strengthening the policymaking process for both provincial and local governments, supporting capacity building in municipalities to promote economic development, and co-designing capacity-building programs for parliamentarians about governance and development issues.

- DFAT funds the Australian Electoral Commission (AEC) to support capacity building for electoral administrations, especially in the Indo-Pacific.[38] The AEC concentrates on providing technical assistance and programs for training and capacity building in the Autonomous Region of Bougainville, Papua New Guinea, the Solomon Islands, Sri Lanka, Tokelau, Tonga, and Vanuatu. DFAT and the AEC also support capacity-building programs through the Pacific Islands, Australia, and New Zealand Electoral Administrators Network to "enhance the capacity of electoral administrators[,] provide a forum of cooperation between members[, and] strengthen Pacific electoral management bodies." The AEC participates in the Building Resources in Governance, Democracy and Elections partnership, a capacity-building program for electoral administrators, including international organizations such as the UN Electoral Assistance Division. The AEC also provides support for international delegations and study tours from 31 nations, including Indonesia, the Philippines, Timor-Leste, and Vanuatu.[39]

Freedom of Expression and the Press

Australia supports the development of a "strong, professional, and sustainable media sector in partner countries in the Indo-Pacific region."[40]

- The DFAT Human Rights NGO Forum is an annual forum that allows NGOs and DFAT to work together on international human rights priorities, including on freedom of expression. Participation in these annual forums by NGOs and civil society organizations (CSOs) helps them engage with multilateral processes, assisting them in developing the capacity to engage on the international stage.[41]

Human Rights

Australia promotes human rights through constructive bilateral dialogue and works to advance human rights through development aid and humanitarian support.[42] When Australia was a member of the UN Human Rights Council (UNHRC) from 2018 to 2020, it was focused on advancing the rights of women and girls; promoting good governance and stronger democratic institutions; promoting and protecting the freedom of expression; advancing human rights for Indigenous peoples around the globe; promoting strong national human rights institutions and capacity building; defending the rights of persons with disabilities; working toward the abolition of the death penalty; campaigning for equal human rights for LGBTQ+ persons; defending freedom of religion or belief; and strengthening civil society participation in UN processes and more generally.[43] The DFAT Human Rights NGO Forum is another platform in which DFAT can engage CSOs and NGOs on human rights issues, such as protections for human rights defenders.[44]

TECHNICAL SUPPORT, DEVELOPMENT ASSISTANCE, AND FOREIGN AID RELATED TO CIVIL SOCIETY

Humanitarian Assistance

- Australia Assists is a government-funded program, managed by international nonprofit organization RedR Australia, that deploys experts to work with governments, multilateral agencies, and communities in response to natural disasters and conflict. The seven-year AUD 80.7 million (approximately $60.8 million) program supports the mobilization and deployment of civilian specialists into various geographic and thematic areas of priority in line with the government's humanitarian responsibilities and national interests.[45]

Development Assistance: Partnerships with the Private Sector and NGOs

- DFAT works with the private sector in two ways: to "embed the private sector as strategic partners in aid programs" and to "enable the private sector to achieve outcomes that promote economic growth and reduce poverty."[46]

- The Direct Aid Program (DAP) is an Australian small grants program that has "the flexibility to work with local communities in developing countries on projects that reduce poverty and achieve sustainable development consistent with Australia's national interest."[47] DAP projects include a wide variety of partners, to include community groups, NGOs, educational institutions, and local governments. In 2020–21, over 270 projects were funded in over 70 countries. DAP projects can receive a maximum of AUD 60,000 (approximately $45,000) over the life of the project and can run up to a maximum of two years.

- Mentioned above, the Australian NGO Cooperation Program (ANCP) is DFAT's largest single support mechanism for Australian NGOs. The program is managed by the NGO Programs, Performance & Quality Section within DFAT. The ANCP supports accredited Australian NGOs through annual grants to help fund and execute their projects. On average, ANCP NGOs deliver more than 400 projects annually in over 50 countries and in a range of sectors, including education, health, water and sanitation, food security, and civil society. In 2019–20, the program contributed AUD 132.5 million (approximately $99.8 million) to projects across the globe; an additional AUD 35.6 million (approximately $26.8 million) came from NGO contributions. Out of the 427 projects in 57 countries, 81 percent were in the Indo-Pacific. To be eligible for ANCP funding, the project must be a co-funded development project and reach beneficiaries from developing countries (found in the OECD DAC list of ODA recipients).[48]

- The Australian Aid: Friendship Grants initiative engages a new and diverse group of partners from across Australia to contribute to Australia's aid program. The Friendship Grants is a three-year AUD 10 million (approximately $7.5 million) program managed by DFAT that provides funding to Australian community organizations in the nonprofit sector for the purpose of delivering effective international development work in the Indo-Pacific.[49]

- The Business Partnerships Platform is DFAT's principal program to accelerate Australia's collaboration with business in addressing regional development challenges. The platform's Covid-19 Recovery Partnerships "support the expansion of inclusive business practices to build more resilient economies and help businesses create livelihood opportunities, enhance gender equality, and support green and resilient economic recovery."[50]

A SAMPLE OF AUSTRALIAN NONGOVERNMENTAL ACTORS INVOLVED IN DEMOCRACY SUPPORT

- The Australian Council for International Development "unites Australia's nongovernment aid and international development organizations to strengthen their collective impact against poverty." Founded in 1965, the council has over 130 members working in 90 developing countries, and it partners with DFAT on a range of initiatives.[51]

- The International Centre for Democratic Partnerships was founded in July 2017 and is an independent nonprofit organization that encourages and facilitates dialogue, discussions, and working relationships among Pacific and Australian leaders in government, civil society, and the private sector. Focusing on common challenges, core priorities include sustainable development and the empowerment of Pacific Island women.[52]

- CARE Australia is an international aid organization that aims to "save lives and defeat poverty," with a special focus on providing equal opportunities for women and girls.[53]

- The International Women's Development Agency has worked for more than 30 years to progress the rights of women and girls. Within the region, the agency works in Cambodia, Myanmar, Timor-Leste, Fiji, the Solomon Islands, and Papua New Guinea and Bougainville.[54]

- Union Aid Abroad–APHEDA is a partnership of Australian unions working for the achievement of dignity at work, social justice, economic equality, and the realization of human rights. The partnership supports stronger union and social movements in Southeast Asia and the Pacific.[55]

OPPORTUNITIES FOR DEMOCRATIC PARTNERSHIP

1. **Bring in partner countries to support local NGOs and civil society groups.** Australia has extensive experience working with local NGOs in developing countries and could share its expertise with countries such as Japan and South Korea that focus more on direct assistance to recipient governments. Australia can help bring other countries to the table in their work with local NGOs to increase the amount of funding and support they receive.

2. **Share knowledge with regional democracies about ways to support domestic NGOs.** In addition to working with local NGOs, Australia has unique programs that provide funding for domestic NGOs, such as the Australian NGO Cooperation Program or Friendship Grants. Moreover, these programs allow Australia to coordinate with a wide variety of NGOs on diverse issues such as human rights, good governance, women's empowerment, and development assistance. Other countries can learn from Australia and adopt similar programs to support their own NGOs, enabling them to provide stronger support for democracy abroad. For example, the DFAT Human Rights NGO Forum provides an opportunity to share knowledge on how to best engage NGOs.

3. **Work with Japan to bolster democracy support efforts in the region.** The deepening relationship between Australia and Japan provides a great opportunity for both countries to collaborate on democracy support activities. Australia can augment its support for women's empowerment and efforts to promote capacity building for legal and judicial institutions with Japanese activities in these areas. Australia and Japan could also coordinate support for the Pacific Islands, a strategic priority for both countries.

JAPAN

"Good Governance Leader"

OVERVIEW

Japan's support for democracy has increased incrementally over the past 20 years, especially since the beginning of the second Abe administration in 2012. Democracy assistance is provided through a "request-based" approach: recipient governments must initiate a request with the Japanese government in order to receive aid. This is integral to the way Japan approaches development cooperation, which is based on three principles: (1) cultivating partnerships with developing countries, (2) encouraging self-help efforts by developing countries, and (3) implementing support through the consultation and consent of recipient countries.

The Japan International Cooperation Agency (JICA) provides bilateral aid to recipient governments in the form of technical cooperation, ODA loans, and grant aid. JICA does provide some support to NGOs through international organizations and relatively small grassroot aid programs, but Japan's request-based approach limits its ability to provide direct support to local NGOs. Due to Japan's lack of cooperation with NGOs, positive effects of ODA are not often visible at the grassroots level. However, Japanese NGOs—such as the Japan NGO Center for International Cooperation (JANIC), Nippon Foundation, and Japan Federation of Bar Associations—play a key role in democracy support abroad.

Japanese ODA mainly focuses on good governance, capacity building, and legal and judicial reform. Key recipient countries in the region include Afghanistan, Indonesia, Vietnam, Cambodia, and Laos. From 2007 to 2016, Japan provided over $2.9 billion in ODA for democracy and governance support, according to OECD data.[56]

BACKGROUND AND RECENT TRENDS

Japan's ODA policy is based on the belief that governance, democracy, and human rights can be indirectly improved in developing countries through economic development. This belief is derived from Japan's experience with successful industrialization after World War II and underscores the critical role of government assistance for Japanese policymakers. Japan's ODA budget is largely focused on infrastructure, which was 64.8 percent of the budget in 2017, as opposed to democracy support, which was 1.9 percent of the budget in 2017. The focus on infrastructure is one way Japan uses development projects to maintain close political relations with recipient countries such as India, ASEAN countries, and others in Asia. As the Japanese government faces tight budget constraints, the visible benefits of infrastructure development projects make it easier for the government to justify the use of public funds for ODA.[57]

Historically, Japan has supported democracy indirectly through the promotion of economic development. At the G7 Lyon Summit in 1996, Japan announced the Partnership for Democratic Development (PDD), which was meant to strengthen cooperation on human rights and democratization. The purpose of the PDD was to achieve democratic development in developing countries through assistance for institutional building in the legislative, governmental, electoral, and mass media sectors.[58]

The percentage of Japanese ODA allocated to democracy-related projects has increased incrementally over the years.[59] Starting in 2006 with the "Arc of Freedom and Prosperity" concept, support for democratic rules and norms became increasingly emphasized in Japanese foreign policy.[60] At the onset of the second Abe administration, the Japanese government expressed support for universal values such as democracy and the rule of law as a priority in the 2013 National Security Strategy.[61] In 2015, the cabinet passed the Development Cooperation Charter, which recognizes the importance of rule of law and democracy and states that Japan will provide assistance for good governance efforts, legal and judicial development, and capacity building for anti-corruption.[62] There are apparent strategic calculations behind Japan's increased underscoring of democracy in its foreign policy, including the maintenance of the maritime status quo in Asia, growing Chinese security concerns, and Japanese efforts to strengthen its influence in the region.[63]

Japanese ODA mainly focuses on projects related to good governance and legal system reform. From 2007 to 2016, most democracy-related ODA went toward "public sector policy and administrative management" (approximately $1.5 billion) and "legal and judicial development" ($976.8 million).[64] While Japan also supports media freedom and free and fair elections, ODA distributed to sectors related to elections and civil society has expanded only on a small scale.[65] Despite the increasing emphasis on democracy support in Japan's ODA policy, the amount of ODA spending on democracy-related projects is limited compared to that of other OECD nations. For example, from 2007 to 2016, Japan's support for government and civil society as a share of its total ODA was on average 2.1 percent—placing it at 26th out of 29 OECD countries.[66]

Japanese nonprofit organizations also provide support for democracy in Asia. For example, JANIC facilitates collaboration between Japanese civil society organizations and counterparts in Asian countries in order to expand civic space and promote the rule of law and fair and equitable sustainable development. In addition, Genron NPO holds symposiums on democracy to foster dialogue among civil society groups in India, Indonesia, and Japan.[67] While it is very limited, there is some government support for these civil society networks; for example, Genron NPO symposiums held in cooperation with Japan's Ministry of Foreign Affairs (MOFA) are funded by the Japan Foundation Asia Center.

GOVERNMENT SUPPORT FOR DEMOCRACY-RELATED INITIATIVES

Good Governance and Administrative Support

Japan provides financial support, trains personnel, hosts trainees, and conducts exchange programs. In 2019, Japanese ODA for "public sector policy and administrative management" was $42 million.[68] Examples include:

- Japan pledged JPY 10 billion (approximately $88 million) in 2006 to establish the ASEAN-based think tank Economic Research Institute for ASEAN and East Asia (ERIA). The purpose of ERIA is to conduct research related to regional integration and support initiatives that expand policy research capacity in the least developed countries in the region. It specifically focuses on expanding the technical expertise of government officials in Cambodia, Laos, Vietnam, and Myanmar.[69]

- In 2013, Japan's Ministry of Internal Affairs and Communications signed an agreement with the Government Inspectorate of Vietnam to cooperate on its capacity to handle the increasing number of claims brought by citizens against the government. The Ministry of Internal Affairs and Communications implemented a three-year training program as part of this agreement, with the program funded by JICA.[70]

- In March 2018, the Japanese government pledged $5.2 million through the United Nations Development Programme (UNDP) for the capacity-building initiative Strengthening Legislators' Capacity in the Pacific Island Countries, which supports the legislatures in Samoa, the Marshall Islands, and Micronesia. In addition, this project increased ongoing Japanese support for the parliaments of the Solomon Islands, Vanuatu, and Fiji. Japan's work to support parliamentary development in the Pacific Islands builds on previous Japanese government support for the region, to include the Fiji Parliament Support Program (2014–2017).[71]

- JICA provides funding for the ASEAN Inter-Parliamentary Assembly (AIPA) through ERIA. In 2016, the AIPA and ERIA signed a memorandum of understanding to cooperate on research and capacity-building programs for AIPA. AIPA helps support ASEAN parliamentary members through promoting cooperation among parliaments of ASEAN member states and holding exchanges with foreign parliaments, including parliamentary exchanges with Japanese legislators.[72]

- The government of Cambodia's Decentralization and De-concentration Reform Program aims to promote good governance through reform of local public administration. JICA is supporting this effort through the Project for Capacity Development on Training Management for Strengthening Sub-National Administrations (Cambodia), which helps Cambodia develop training programs and teaching materials for local administration personnel in the Ministry of Interior and Sub-National Administration. In addition, this project aims to strengthen the Training Department of the General Department of Administration in Cambodia, so that it can bolster its training strategies and programs. JICA support is actively enhancing the capacity of training management within Cambodian local administration.[73]

Gender and Development

JICA cooperates with countries to create policies and systems that promote gender equality and to boost women and girls' empowerment through activities such as support for maternal and child health promotion, education for women, female entrepreneurs, capacity building to cope with violence against women and girls, and security and training for victims of human trafficking.[74] Examples include:

- JICA has been working with the UNDP since 2014 to develop the capacity of Afghan women police officers to appropriately address gender-based violence cases as part of its Initiative to Develop the Capacity of Female Police Officers to Address Gender-Based Violence (GBV). In 2017 and 2019, JICA invited a total of 22 mid-ranked female officers from Afghanistan to Japan to further strengthen their capacity to address GBV, including how to provide gender-responsive support to survivors.[75]

- JICA hosts training programs in Japan and brings select individuals from foreign governments to acquire knowledge in the field of gender and women's international development. One program is the Seminar for Promotion of Gender Equality III, which aims to "strengthen the capacity of national machinery for gender equality in respective countries and to establish a network of national machineries among Japan and the countries."[76] Another seminar aims to increase the capability of government offices to introduce "gender mainstreaming" in decisionmaking through development activities and case studies in Asia.[77]

Legal and Judicial Reform Assistance

Japan supports the drafting of civil, criminal, and commercial codes; organizes seminars and training for judicial personnel; dispatches Japanese experts (long and short term) to recipient countries; and hosts study visits to Japan.[78] Japan's Ministry of Justice also sends experts and hosts programs for judicial personnel training, often in cooperation with nonprofit entities such as the International Civil and Commercial Law Centre (ICCLC) and the Japan Federation of Bar Associations (JFBA).[79] In 2019, Japanese ODA for "legal and judicial development" totaled $129 million.[80] Projects and initiatives by country are as follows:

CAMBODIA

Historically, JICA has provided assistance in training Cambodia's judges, public prosecutors, and practicing lawyers.[81] In 1999, Cambodia turned to Japan for help with drafting a new civil code and code of civil procedure, which was the catalyst for the Legal and Judicial Development Project.[82]

JICA is currently involved in helping support Cambodia's Civil Code. After the civil procedure code and civil code were promulgated in 2006 and 2007, respectively, JICA began work on implementation. Three projects were launched during this time: the Legal and Judicial Development Project, the Project for Improvement of Training on Civil Matters at the Royal School of Judges and Prosecutors, and the Legal and Judicial Cooperation for the Bar Association of the Kingdom of Cambodia.[83] However, in 2012, JICA instead created a new project titled Legal and Judicial Development Project (Phase IV) to integrate these three projects to cooperate more efficiently.[84]

Japan is currently in its fifth iteration of the Legal and Judicial Development Project. Launched in April 2017, this five-year project is meant to improve the application of the Civil Code and the Code of Civil Procedure. It has three main pillars: developing related legislation, producing forms to be used for civil procedures, and publishing court judgments.[85] The ICCLC, a private-sector Japanese foundation, has helped manage these projects.[86]

VIETNAM

In 1996, Japan started providing ODA to Vietnam for legal and judicial reform in support of the country's Doi Moi (Open Door) policy.[87] JICA helps to train Vietnamese officials by sending experts—including Japanese judges, public prosecutors, and practicing lawyers—to Vietnam. Japan's assistance also includes support for criminal and administrative justice reform, including the law on crimes against the state.[88]

- The purpose of the Project for Harmonized, Practical Legislation and Uniform Application of Law Targeting Year 2020 (April 2015–March 2020) was to establish methods and systems for examination of legal normative documents in Vietnam, as well as to establish review and law enforcement monitoring of legal normative documents at the Ministry of Justice. This was to ensure consistency and uniform implementation and application of legal normative documents. The project also aimed to establish a foundation for the implementation of civil code-related legal normative documents and court practice on civil and criminal cases.[89]

- JICA's newest judicial development project in Vietnam is the Project for Enhancing the Quality and Efficiency of Developing and Implementing Laws in Vietnam. This project is expected to run from January 2021 to 2025 with support from the ICCLC.[90]

MYANMAR

In 2016, JICA provided $1 million in funding support to Rule of Law Centers in Myanmar. These centers were established in Yangon, Mandalay, Myitkyina (Kachin State), and Taunggyi (Shan State) and are "designed to help legal professionals, community leaders, and civil society organizations access and share knowledge, develop skills, and raise awareness of the law."[91]

Another example of a JICA initiative in Myanmar is the Project for Capacity Development of Legal, Judicial, and Relevant Sectors, which was funded from 2013 to 2018. The aim of the project was to "provide support for improving the legislative-screening capabilities in Myanmar's Union Attorney General's Office and the legislative-drafting capabilities in the Supreme Court of the Union, while undertaking activities to draft and revise economic law in Myanmar." JICA provided support for improving the basis of human resources development for prosecutors, judges, and other officials at both the Attorney General's Office and the supreme court. In addition, JICA helped examine the consistency of targeted laws and regulations. As part of this project, JICA conducted training in Japan in March 2015 to introduce the legislative processes of Japan and other countries to Myanmar participants. Through discussions with Japanese experts, participants were able to examine the most suitable processes for Myanmar.[92]

LAOS

The Legal and Judicial Development Project was started by JICA in Laos in 2003 for the purpose of upgrading the basic legal skills of Laotians working in the law and justice fields. This included providing textbooks, compiling legal databases, and creating manuals.[93]

Working with the National University of Laos, Ministry of Justice, People's Supreme Court, and Office of the

Supreme People's Prosecutor, JICA created a joint working group, called the Project for Human Resource Development in the Legal Sector (2010–2014), to develop a common understanding of Laotian law across organizational boundaries. The group also studied where the law could be improved, and JICA provided support with drafting a civil code midway through the project.[94]

Phase II of the Project for Human Resource Development in the Legal Sector (2014–2018) deepened and broadened the understanding of Laotian law through involving the Lao Bar Association and police. JICA continued its assistance in drafting a civil code as well as compiling documentation on civil, economic, and criminal law. JICA also helped develop a legal training program for Laos.[95]

MONGOLIA

Japan has supported legal and judicial development in Mongolia since 2004; most recently, it has helped lay the groundwork for Mongolia's adoption of a court mediation system.

- Japan provided technical support to help with the adoption of a court mediation system through the Project for Strengthening the Mediation System (2010–2012). "It helped train mediators, promoted awareness of the mediation systems, strengthened the operation capacity of the Association of Mongolian Advocate's mediation center, and assisted with drafting a mediation law."[96]

- In phase two of the Project for Strengthening the Mediation System (2013–2015), Japan provided assistance for mediator training and institutional development following the enactment of the mediation law. This helped to prepare for the rollout of the mediation system at trial courts throughout Mongolia.[97]

NEPAL

Japan began engaging with Nepal in 2009 when JICA launched the Democratization Process Support Program.[98] Since then, Japan has conducted trainings within Nepal, dispatched legal support advisers to Nepal, and helped draft and implement a civil code.[99]

- JICA dispatched advisers to help the Supreme Court of Nepal through the Legal Support Advisor (2010–2019) program to implement the second and third five-year strategic plans for the judiciary more effectively and efficiently. These advisers also helped support the process of enacting and disseminating the Civil Code and aided with judicial mediation.[100]

- The Project for Strengthening the Capacity of Court for Expeditious and Reliable Dispute Settlement (2013–2018) aimed to "enhance the function of courts in settling disputes expeditiously and impartially," improve the court system's management of contentious cases, and "encourage settlement of disputes by judicial mediation."[101]

Election Support

Japan provides financial support, materials, equipment, training, and observers to support elections.

- From 2015 to 2017, JICA provided a grant to the UNDP of JPY 740 million (approximately $6.5 million) to support fair and transparent elections in Kyrgyzstan by providing equipment to verify voter identity and conducting a training-the-trainers program on usage of the system.[102]

- JICA has supported general elections in Cambodia every five years since 1993 by sending equipment and monitors. Recent JICA technical cooperation also includes assistance for better organization of the general elections.[103]

Free Press

Japan has emphasized media assistance with the long-term aim of promoting democracy. However, this assistance is primarily offered to state-owned media.[104] Examples include:

- From 2010 to 2013, JICA supported Nepal's Ministry of Information and Communications as part of its Project for Promoting Peace Building and Democratization through Capacity Development of the Media Sector in Nepal. This included support for drafting a revised media policy, legislation, regulations, and guidelines. It also supported Radio Nepal's transformation into a public service broadcaster.[105]

TECHNICAL SUPPORT, DEVELOPMENT ASSISTANCE, AND FOREIGN AID RELATED TO CIVIL SOCIETY

Government Assistance for Japanese NGOs

- Under the Grant Assistance for Grass-Roots Human Security Projects program, Japanese embassies in developing countries can fund up to $100,000 in grants to local NGOs for humanitarian activities, but they can only fund tangible items such as medical equipment.[106]

- The JICA Partnership Program can fund Japanese NGOs in developing countries, but the amount is limited to 1.5 percent of the total funding for NGOs in the ODA budget.[107]

Human Resources Development

- Through the JICA Development Studies Program, JICA aims to strengthen long-term training programs (Knowledge Co-Creation Programs) for future leaders and administrative officials who play a key role in national management. Through trainings and studies, scholars can deepen their understanding of topics such as politics, law, governance, economics, finance, industrial development, management, and technological innovation.[108]

- The Pacific Leaders' Educational Assistance for Development of State (Pacific-LEADS) program was created to train junior officials from the Pacific Islands. In 2019, 40 JICA scholars completed courses under the Pacific-LEADS program to develop skills for leading development initiatives in their respective countries. The SDGs Global Leadership Program, the successor to the Pacific-LEADS program, allows Pacific Island scholars to experience internships at government agencies or private companies in Japan, which creates mutual learning opportunities for both sides.[109]

A SAMPLE OF JAPANESE NONGOVERNMENTAL ACTORS INVOLVED IN DEMOCRACY SUPPORT

Japan NGO Center for International Cooperation (JANIC)

JANIC is active in mobilizing international cooperation for democracy support and advocates for democracy and human rights in the Indo-Pacific region. It plays a central role in coordinating promotion of the rule of law, transparent government, and UN Sustainable Development Goal (SDG) 16 in Asian countries.

- The Civil 20 (C20) Civil Society Platform is an engagement group through which CSOs can contribute to the G20. JANIC served as the joint secretariat of Japan Civil Society Platform for the 2019 G20 Summit, together with the Japan Civil Society Network on SDGs.[110] The Civil Society Platform will continue to work with Asian partners to defend civic space, advocate for human rights, and promote inclusive development as Indonesia prepares to chair the G20 in 2022.

- JANIC organized the first Tokyo Democracy Forum in April 2019 in partnership with the Asian Democracy Network and other Asian NGOs as part of the C20 summit. At the first Tokyo Democracy Forum, the C20 adopted the "Tokyo Declaration on Peace, Human Rights and Democratic Governance: Towards Improvement of Civic Space for the SDG 16+."[111] The second forum was held in February 2021 and focused on the impact of Covid-19 on human rights, democracy, and civil society.[112] JANIC is conducting a major survey on the impacts of Covid-19 on freedom of expression and the press, restriction on movement, civic space, and human rights in Asian countries in a preparation for the third forum to be held in February 2022.[113]

Japan Federation of Bar Associations (JFBA)

The JFBA promotes the rule of law by providing international legal assistance. The JFBA partners with JICA to implement legal and judicial development projects, including sending experts abroad for local training seminars and helping plan and implement training programs in Japan. JFBA also assists bar associations in developing countries, organizes a conference on access to justice in Asia, provides information and training to lawyers in Japan, and organizes seminars on international legal assistance. JFBA has signed friendship agreements with a total of 14 foreign and international bar associations, including Cambodia (2000), Vietnam (2013), and Mongolia (2017).[114]

International Civil and Commercial Law Center

The ICCLC is a private-sector Japanese foundation that helps Asian countries develop legal infrastructures. It engages with regional partners by "organizing symposia and seminars, conducting research, and sharing information to reach a better common understanding of the legal system as it applies to cross-border economic transactions."[115] The ICCLC supports JICA by accepting foreign trainees and organizing advisory group meetings as a major Japanese partner in JICA's legal and judicial development programs. The ICCLC also organizes the Japan-China Civil and Commercial Law Seminar, holds seminars on other subjects related to legal development, and researches Asian countries' civil and commercial legislation.[116]

University of Nagoya Center for Asian Legal Exchange

The University of Nagoya, through the Center for Asian Legal Exchange (CALE), has operated its Research and Deduction Center on Japanese law in seven Asian developing countries and trained law students on the rule of law.[117] CALE's mission is to "conduct theoretical research on the law and legal assistance programs in Asia," "train legal professionals in Asian countries," and "mentor global leaders who will contribute to Asia's development."[118] CALE's main activities include supporting JICA's legal and judicial development projects as a major Japanese partner; educating students from the region under JICA human resource development programs; conducting research on Asian law and legal development programs; creating research and education centers for Japanese law in the region; collaborating with Japanese and overseas institutions in the field of legal assistance and Asia law; and organizing research seminars, symposia, and international conferences.[119]

Research centers have been established at the following universities:

- Tashkent State University of Law (2005)
- National University of Mongolia (2006)
- Hanoi Law University (2007)
- Royal University of Law and Economics in Cambodia (2008)
- Ho Chi Minh City Law University (2012)
- University of Yangon (2013)
- National University of Laos (2014)
- University of Gadjah Mada (2014)[120]

Genron NPO

Genron NPO holds "democracy dialogues," which are symposiums on democracy that feature voices from around the Asia Pacific, as well as hosts its own Tokyo Conference on Democracy.[121] In 2021, the annual Tokyo Conference featured democracy and Covid-19 as its theme ("putting democracy back in the hands of the people").[122]

The Nippon Foundation

The Nippon Foundation supports democracy through its human resources development projects. Specifically, it has hosted a military officials exchange program since 2014 between the Myanmar Defense Services and Japanese Self-Defense Forces to "exchange ideas of what an army should be like in a democratic nation."[123] Other programs support training for officials of the Ministry of Border Affairs (2016–present), officials of the General Administration Department (2020–present), and regional administrative officials (2020–present). Examples of programs include:

- The Japan-Myanmar Military Officials Exchange Program;
- Training for officials of the Ministry of Border Affairs;
- Training for officials of the General Administration Department, including for all state and regional governments; and
- Training for Myanmar regional administrative officials.

OPPORTUNITIES FOR DEMOCRATIC PARTNERSHIP

1. **Work with other democracies to increase support to local NGOs.** Because of Japan's request-based approach, it is hard for JICA to contribute directly to civil society in developing countries. Japan should work with countries such as Australia and the United States who have more experience working with local NGOs. In addition, Japan should explore ways to fund local civil society groups by funding NGOs already working in different countries.

2. **Coordinate democracy support with other Quad members.** The Quad is first and foremost a partnership of democracies that is committed to advancing democratic norms and values in the Indo-Pacific region. This goal is apparent in the countries' cooperation on development assistance, humanitarian aid, and efforts to counter disinformation. More quadrilateral cooperation on training, elections, judicial development, women's empowerment, and other aspects of democracy support would strengthen each individual country's activities in these areas and allow for new opportunities to collaborate. Japan is in an opportune position to lead on many of these issues, especially in the legal and judicial space, and should leverage its positive relationships with Australia and India to coordinate a multilateral effort.

3. **Collaborate with the United States on the democracy summit's "year of action."** Japan and

the United States share a commitment to universal values and common principles including freedom, democracy, human rights, and the rule of law. Japan should shape the agenda for the Biden administration's "year of action" following the virtual democracy summit in December 2021. Japan can coordinate with other countries on regional activities and bring an Asian voice to the table to make U.S. efforts more inclusive of Asian countries.

INDIA

"Election Expert"

OVERVIEW

Since its founding, India has been a supporter of democracy movements around the world, though often through the lens of decolonization. However, support was often overshadowed by India's status as a recipient of foreign aid up until the turn of the century. In the early 2000s, India began developing its aid program and providing external support for developing countries. In recent years, India has begun to focus more on democracy support, good governance, and transparent development in response to China's Belt and Road Initiative (BRI). India rarely mentions democracy explicitly when characterizing its aid initiatives, but this shift in emphasis can be seen as a result of growing financial resources and greater socialization with Western and Asian democracies, especially since joining the Quad.

Indian bilateral foreign aid conducted through the Ministry of External Affairs (MEA) is generally focused on infrastructure development, market access, and election infrastructure. The most prominent form of support for democracy is for training and resources to help other nations facilitate free, fair, and accessible elections. Indian aid is only offered by invitation, following the values of respecting individual states' sovereignty. While India generally employs a request-based approach, in rare cases it may have contact with ethnic minorities in countries such as Sri Lanka or Nepal. Within Asia, a large portion of Indian grant aid goes to South Asian countries such as Bhutan, Afghanistan, Nepal, and Bangladesh, but India also provides aid to other regional countries, such as Myanmar and Mongolia.

BACKGROUND AND RECENT TRENDS

India is the largest democracy in the world, with a population of over 1.3 billion people. It has nearly 900 million eligible voters, with national elections divided into seven phases over 38 days.[124] India's experience facilitating large elections lends itself to democracy support focused primarily on providing assistance for monitoring and facilitating elections in other countries.[125] India also touts its own experience as the world's largest democracy and believes that the best way it can promote democracy and human rights abroad is to highlight its own success as a great nation that cherishes both.[126] India's economic development can also demonstrate that democracy and freedom are important to economic growth and provide the developing world with an alternative to the Chinese model of authoritarianism, even if India does not characterize its support for democracy in such terms.[127]

India's stance on democracy support can be contradictory. Because of India's focus on non-alignment and sovereignty, India describes its actions in terms of "democracy assistance" or "support" rather than "democracy promotion."[128] Similarly, India's foreign affairs strategy "excludes ideas such as exporting democracy."[129] For example, it avoided listing democracy as a priority for India in the foreign secretary's September 2012 address to the 67th UN General Assembly.[130] However, India participates in multilateral signaling in favor of democracy in the United Nations, provided it does not individually target non-democratic nations.[131] From 2006 to 2015, India's financial contributions to the UN Democracy Fund (UNDEF) totaled $31.5 million, funding 66 NGO-led projects in Afghanistan, Bangladesh, Bhutan, Myanmar, the Maldives, Nepal, Pakistan, and Sri Lanka.[132] Contributions to the UNDEF have declined under the current government led by Narendra Modi, though India currently remains the third-highest donor to the fund.[133]

The main agency for facilitating development assistance is India's MEA, which focuses on socioeconomic development assistance, technical training, and capacity building through programs such as the Indian Technical and Economic Cooperation program.[134] When compared to India's spending on socioeconomic development issues, India's bilateral and multilateral financial support for democracy-related projects across South Asia is significant lower—its donations of $31.5 million to the UNDEF over a decade are overshadowed by its development assistance budget of $1.15 billion for the single fiscal year of 2015–16.[135] In addition, like Japan, India only provides democracy assistance when requested and generally provides aid to sovereign states and state institutions rather than supporting civil society groups.[136] When India does provide bilateral aid, it focuses less on democratic norms and more on education and technical assistance.[137] Furthermore, Indian funding for NGOs working on democracy is distributed through UNDEF to avoid perceptions of interference.

India's increasing interest in democracy support in the region has been theorized to be a result of alignment between democracy's spread and its consolidation with Indian economic and security interests, especially in Southeast Asia, as well as impacted by "concerns about China's growing influence in its neighborhood."[138] China's aggressive attempts to exert influence across Asia are forcing India to reassess its "non-aligned" policy. Though India's democracy assistance in the region may be fueled by China, India takes the view that norm-driven policies may make it harder to engage. Therefore, despite India's own democratic example and its preference toward democracy as a desirable regime form, it is unlikely to be active in explicit democracy "promotion."[139]

It is difficult to get the full picture of India's development assistance and calculate how much it spends, as it is not a member of the OECD or the DAC. The government of India publishes its Union Budget annually, but the section on budgetary allocations for grants and loans to foreign governments does not specifically mention democracy or democracy-related categories.[140] The MEA similarly publishes its annual reports, but financing and budget data pertains only to technical and economic cooperation and does not specifically mention democracy or democracy-related categories.[141] However, it is still useful to put into perspective India's total aid to foreign countries, as well as aid to important Asian partners. India's total aid to foreign countries for FY 2020–21 was approximately 69 billion rupees (a little under $1 billion), with approximately 42 percent of aid going to Bhutan and 12 percent going to Nepal.[142]

GOVERNMENT SUPPORT FOR DEMOCRACY-RELATED INITIATIVES

Women's Empowerment

- The Indian government, donors, philanthropists, and corporations partner with the U.S. Agency for International Development (USAID) to promote programming to help women, men, girls, boys, and transgender individuals to address social inequalities.[143]

- The partnership on Expanding Access to Health Care, Responding to Gender-Based Violence and Empowering Adolescent Girls seeks to implement interventions that allow individuals to gain better access to health and family-planning services and education. The program is also working to sensitize young people about harmful gender norms to reduce domestic and intimate-partner violence.[144]

- The partnership on Promoting Women's Empowerment works to help rural women improve their livelihoods with innovative techniques to increase the supply and affordability of fish and fish products. This program also trains women to be health workers and health entrepreneurs, providing trusted hands to bring medical technologies into their communities.[145]

Free and Fair Elections through India's Election Commission

- India promotes itself as a global authority on electoral systems as the "largest practicing democracy in the world with over 60 years record of holding effective, transparent, and credible elections."[146]

- India is working to be a hub for democratic electoral management exchanges and training programs.[147] It sends resources to aid in democracy promotion and electoral support to willing countries in the Arab world, Africa, and Central and South Asia.

- India's Election Commission promotes inter-institutional contacts and provides technical support and resources to foreign election authorities only on request. In this way, the Indian government promotes best practices of systems, but not democracy as a universal best practice.[148]

- The Indo-U.S. Joint Declaration from 2010 outlined an international partnership for democracy and development. The agreement outlined terms to explore cooperation in supporting and strengthening election organization and management in other interested countries.[149]

- The Election Commission of India established the Indian International Institute of Democracy and Election Management (IIDEM) in June 2011. The IIDEM is an advanced resource center of learning, research, and training on participatory democracy and election management. The IIDEM has helped train officials from about 50 countries, mostly in sub-Saharan Africa.[150]

- Within the region, India's efforts have been most prominently focused on South Asia and on supporting unstable democracies. India has provided ongoing bilateral assistance to democratic institutions in Afghanistan and has intervened in Nepal's constitutional disputes. In addition, it worked to bring about new elections after a "quasi-coup" in the Maldives and performed mediation in Bangladesh's electoral conflict.[151]

Capacity Building, Training, and Legal and Judicial Development

Indian aid has historically been focused on providing technical assistance, given its proven capacities in federal management between the central and state government systems. Capacity building and skills development are the centerpieces of India's cooperation plans and represent a non-confrontational effort to build internal relationships.[152]

- One major example of India's technical assistance is the Indian Technical and Economic Cooperation (ITEC) program, which serves to help other countries to develop their technology competencies. Launched in 1964 with the Special Commonwealth Assistance for Africa Program and the Colombo Plan, the MEA and IIDEM hold ongoing Capacity Development trainings for ITEC countries. Africa is the largest recipient of assistance through India's ITEC program.[153]

- The MEA set up the Development Partnership Administration to coordinate India's development cooperation activities. It has connected 47 Indian institutions conducting training programs to over 160 countries of the world in various capacity-building fields, such as entrepreneurship development, business management, information technology, vocational training, and foreign service training.[154]

- The MEA trained 1,800 Bangladesh Civil Service officials in 2019 at the National Centre for Good Governance in Mussoorie.[155]

- India's total assistance to Afghanistan in support of infrastructure, institutions, and capacity building for local government has exceeded $2 billion.[156] For example, Indian financial and organizational support was used to construct Afghanistan's Parliament House and Selma Dam, as well as to provide training to Afghan administration, farming, health, and education.[157]

Judicial development trainings are also conducted directly by India's parliament. Specifically, the Parliamentary Research and Training Institute for Democracies (PRIDE), formerly known as the Bureau of Parliamentary Studies and Training, conducts annual international training programs.[158] International training programs for foreign parliamentary officials include the Parliamentary Internship Programme and the International Training Programme in Legislative Drafting. PRIDE also supports short-duration study visits for members of foreign parliaments, government officials, scholars, students, and others. Participants for the international training programs are drawn from countries covered under ITEC, funded by the MEA. Lastly, PRIDE conducts Attachment Programmes for parliamentary or government officials of foreign countries, which are customized and ad hoc in nature.

- The Parliamentary Internship Programme provides participants with opportunities to exchange ideas and experiences, as well as learn about the traditions, culture, and working of parliamentary institutions in India. The most recent iteration (the 35th Parliamentary Internship Programme for Foreign Parliamentary Officials) took place from September 2, 2019, to October 1, 2019, and included Asian participants from Afghanistan, Mongolia, Sri Lanka, Myanmar, Nepal, the Maldives, and Bhutan.[159]

- The International Training Programme in Legislative Drafting provides participants with the necessary skills, concepts, and techniques for drafting legislation. The most recent iteration (the 35th International Training Program in Legislative Drafting) took place from January 15 to February 14, 2020, and it included Asian participants from Sri Lanka, Myanmar, Fiji, Bangladesh, Bhutan, Nepal, and the Maldives.[160]

TECHNICAL SUPPORT, DEVELOPMENT ASSISTANCE, AND FOREIGN AID RELATED TO CIVIL SOCIETY

Humanitarian Assistance

- More than two-thirds of India's humanitarian assistance is directed to South Asia. Past examples include "first response" efforts for the 2004 tsunami, the 2005 India-Pakistan earthquake, cyclones Nargis and Mora in 2008 and 2017, the 2014 water crisis in the Maldives, and the Rohingya crisis in 2018.[161]

- This "first responder" title indicates India's effort to be a leading actor in Asia, countering potential influence and resources from Chinese aid. India's role as a regional first responder was actualized during Operation Maitri, the response to the 2015 Nepal earthquake that included coordination between the Indian army, air force, and other specialized teams.[162]

Infrastructure

- Half of the Indian government's economic assistance in Asia goes to infrastructure (roads, roadways, ports, and other projects).[163] This represents the key national goal of connecting Indian goods and services to other nations and accelerating regional integration.

- MEA and public sector enterprises often partner to create infrastructure projects, primarily focusing on Nepal, Bangladesh, Bhutan, and Myanmar.

Technical Assistance, Education, and Technology Support

- The Indian Institutes of Technology (IITs) are centers of advanced learning and among the first Indian higher-education institutions to create industrial liaisons and technology transfer offices. MEA uses IITs for feasibility studies, sending experts abroad to support ongoing or future projects.[164]

- The Indira Gandhi National Open University is a network of 47 regional centers that includes 1,200 study centers in India and a further 200 across 38 countries.[165] These study centers offer undergraduate and graduate educations as well as professional development courses.

- The National Small Industries Corporation promotes small-scale industry in India by creating international connections.[166] The effort is commissioned by MEA to establish training courses to benefit small-scale industry, particularly in rural areas. The focus competency areas include identifying technology, securing raw material, training labor, and assisting in the hiring and purchase of machinery.

- Since 2003, the government of India has extended lines of credit (LOCs) for development assistance through the India Exim Bank to developing partner countries. The MEA's Development Partnership Administration Division is responsible for India's development assistance programs abroad and oversees the LOCs routed through the India Exim Bank. According to the bank's Operative LOC, India is engaging with Mongolia for joint information technology education and development of institutions, infrastructure, and human resources in Mongolia. One example is the Indo-Mongolia Joint Information Technology Education & Outsourcing Center Project, which is valued at $20 million, though this money is not yet available for procurement. Another example is the Development of Institutions, Infrastructure and Human Resources in Mongolia Project, which is valued at $1 billion and is available for procurement.[167]

OPPORTUNITIES FOR DEMOCRATIC PARTNERSHIP

1. **Collaborate with regional partners on support for free and fair elections.** India's strongest area of democracy support is in training, especially when it comes to implementing elections. Therefore, India should work with Quad countries such as Australia and Japan to increase their support for election capacity building. Specifically, countries can help fund the Indian International Institute of Democracy and Election Management, which conducts trainings in the region and sends experts to learn from India's expertise.

2. **Increase support for women's empowerment at home and abroad.** India scores poorly in global surveys of gender equality in both economic and political empowerment. However, India is trying to make domestic improvements while working with USAID to promote women's empowerment abroad. India should continue to close the gender gap at home and work with regional countries—in addition to the United States—that have more expertise in this field.

INDONESIA
"ASEAN Organizer"

OVERVIEW

Since 1998, democracy has become an important component of Indonesia's foreign policy outlook. This manifested in the creation of the Bali Democracy Forum (BDF) and bilateral efforts with other countries on anti-corruption and judicial reform. Most importantly, this focus on democracy was apparent in Indonesia's efforts within ASEAN, culminating in the passage of the ASEAN Declaration of Human Rights in 2012. Indonesia's legitimacy as a democracy-supporting actor in the region relies on its status as Southeast Asia's most stable democracy. Drawing from the example of its own democratic development, Indonesia's brand of democracy promotion is pragmatic, context-specific, and non-interventionist. Like other countries in the region, Indonesia's aid is development-oriented, and its support for democratic principles has historically been characterized by development and technical assistance in areas such as agriculture, fisheries, microfinance, and public health. Though the government has provided more direct democracy support in recent years, Indonesia's approach is best summarized as democracy promotion through development.

The primary tools available to Indonesia are its convening power and its outsized role in multilateral institutions such as the BDF. Indonesia also directly funds the Institute for Peace and Democracy (IPD), which is primarily responsible for running BDF and related forums and engaging civil society in the region. Indonesia's outward-facing democracy support is largely focused on good governance, capacity building, and civil society, and its portfolio was recently expanded to include free press and democracy crisis response. However, Indonesia's efforts to support democracy are not always transparent. Indonesia is a member of the OECD, but it is not a member, observer, or participant in OECD's DAC, which tracks official ODA.

BACKGROUND AND RECENT TRENDS

Indonesia's experience with democracy is unique and contrasts sharply with Western ideas of liberal democracy. Pockets of religious extremism and discrimination against ethnic minorities persist. Yet Indonesia remains Southeast Asia's most stable democracy and a guiding light for developing countries in the region and the world. As the fourth-largest country in the world by population and the world's largest Muslim-majority country, Indonesia is a testament to the fact that democracy can thrive anywhere and stands in defiance of stereotypes that Asian values or Islam are incompatible with democracy.[168] Indonesia also represents an alternative path for emerging powers to follow—one that does not emphasize economic might and military capabilities, but instead focuses on democracy, development, and stability by pursuing a foreign policy of restraint with its neighbors and active engagement with the world.[169] Indonesia's efforts to support democracy in the region therefore stem from the power of its example as a functioning, diverse, non-Western democracy.[170]

Indonesia started to include democracy in its foreign policy outlook in 1998. At the behest of the Ministry of Foreign Affairs, Indonesia began to consolidate its various technical cooperation programs under a common umbrella to increase their effectiveness. Indonesia's democracy promotion efforts were most prominent from 2004 to 2014, when President Susilo Bambang Yudhoyono deliberately made democracy promotion a prominent feature of his foreign policy. Hassan Wirajuda and Marty Natalegawa, Yudhoyono's foreign ministers, carried out that mission. Pak Hassan largely conceptualized the role of Indonesia as a democracy promoter. He asserted that Indonesia's role as a diverse, Muslim-majority democracy in Asia meant that these various non-Western identities were compatible with democracy. Pak Hassan also pushed for the inclusion of democracy and human rights within ASEAN. In 2007, the ASEAN Charter included commitments to adhere to and strengthen democracy, good governance, rule of law, and human rights.[171] Pak Hassan's push for an ASEAN human rights body in Article 14 of the charter later evolved into what is now known as the ASEAN Intergovernmental Commission on Human Rights.[172] It was also under Pak Hassan's tenure that the BDF and IPD were created, both key pillars of Indonesia's democracy support in the region.

Pak Marty built on Pak Hassan's work of establishing Indonesia as a democracy promoter by reconciling Indonesian democracy promotion with the country's non-interventionist founding principles. In 2012, he succeeded in securing the passage of the ASEAN Declaration of Human Rights, and his work to find consensus on this declaration remains a landmark achievement of Indonesian democracy promotion in the region.[173] During this time, Indonesia also engaged in third-party collaboration with countries such as Australia, Japan, the United Kingdom, and Germany to secure funds for Indonesia's democracy support efforts. This allowed Indonesia to execute projects on electoral democracy, interfaith dialogue, and other democratic values with limited government resources.

Indonesia's current president, Joko "Jokowi" Widodo, has largely retreated from the international scene, preferring to focus on domestic issues, and has not emphasized democracy in his foreign policy.[174] However, Indonesia's role as a Muslim-majority democracy continues to power its foreign policy. Indonesia's Muslims by and large want Jokowi to stand up for the Rohingya, and in the wake of the coup in Myanmar on February 1, 2021, Jokowi mentioned the importance of rule of law, good governance, human rights, and democracy.[175] Indonesia's experience as a leading democracy and its convening power within ASEAN and the Indo-Pacific greatly contributes to democracy support in the region. Through institutional initiatives such as the BDF, Indonesia's support for democratic principles persists and even has potential to grow via cooperation with other like-minded countries in the region.

Indonesia does not have significant financial resources to commit to democracy support, nor does this information appear readily in the country's ledgers. Tracking Indonesia's ODA to other countries is extremely challenging due to the opaque nature of its documentation system. While Indonesia is a member of the OECD, it is not a member, observer, or associate of the OECD's DAC (a body that tracks ODA, some of which is dedicated to democracy support). While Indonesia is listed as a recipient of ODA, the DAC does not track Indonesia as a donor country.

GOVERNMENT SUPPORT FOR DEMOCRACY-RELATED INITIATIVES

The Bali Democracy Forum

The BDF is a meeting held in Bali, attended by representatives from nations in the Asia-Pacific region. The forum was initiated by Indonesia in 2008 with the stated aim of fostering democracy, human rights, equality, and mutual respect.[176] According to former foreign minister Marty Natalegawa, the forum is the "sole platform for intergovernmental dialogue and cooperation in political development in Asia."[177] Below are some key traits of the forum.

- The BDF represents an Indonesian approach in democracy promotion that is distinct from that of Western countries. Promoting a "home-grown democracy" represents a culture of tolerance and harmony—inherent features of Asian interstate relations. However, Indonesia is still constrained by regional norms of noninterference that respect the domestic affairs of other countries.[178]
- Democracy has become part of the national identity of Indonesia in the post-Suharto era. Indonesian democracy promotion in the BDF is best explained by the concept of identity, rather than a matter of national security, as has been the case for Western countries.[179]
- The BDF is consultative by nature, which reduces the forcefulness of Indonesian democracy support. Its inclusive nature and emphasis on tolerance remains an important pillar in Indonesian support for democracy.[180]

The Institute for Peace and Democracy

The IPD, which is independent from the government in terms of its management and funding, was formed by the Indonesian Foreign Ministry in 2008 with the support of the state-run Udayana University. It was originally formed to implement the BDF. Recently, though, the organization has been transformed into a fully independent institution and has organized different activities, discussions, and forums related to promotion of peace and democracy.[181]

The IPD, through its support to the BDF, helps host the Bali Civil Society and Media Forum (BCSMF), which focuses on dialogue between civil society and the media. The BCSMF is held as a collaboration between the Ministry of Foreign Affairs (MOFA) and the IPD. Supporting institutions change yearly; in 2020, the forum was supported by the Indonesian Press Council, International IDEA, Friedrich Ebert Stiftung, Westminster Foundation for Democracy, Asia Democracy Network, and Asia Democracy Research Network. The forum does not provide direct financial support for civil society or media. Instead, the aim is to share, reinforce, and spread norms related to protecting civil society and free speech. The 2020 forum was attended by experts, academics, media actors, and activists from national and international civil society organizations from 18 countries, including Australia, Bahrain, Cambodia, Germany, India, Indonesia, Japan, Malaysia, and Myanmar. It focused largely on the intersection of civil society, democracy, and the Covid-19 pandemic, emphasizing that human rights must be protected and that the media has a special role in combating disinformation related to the virus.[182]

The IPD holds several meetings, dialogues, and conferences every year (although it has stopped updating its website with these events as of 2018). The IPD has hosted and convened events on elections, media, gender, pluralism, and other democracy-related topics, mostly focused on Cambodia, Laos, Myanmar, and Vietnam.

Myanmar

Over the past decade, Indonesia has emerged as an important actor in Myanmar diplomacy, both bilaterally and multilaterally as a prominent member of ASEAN. Indonesia's goal in its engagement with Myanmar has been to "share" its own experience of transition from semi-authoritarian rule and its handling of various internal armed conflicts to help promote best practices. Indonesia has cooperated with Myanmar on initiatives for peace and security training in response to the demand of the government in Myanmar.[183]

- Indonesia's peacebuilding engagement in Myanmar has included activities aimed at sharing best practices and discussing Indonesia's mistakes of the past so that they are not repeated in Myanmar. Topics touched on include military reform, election processes, capacity building for parliament and political parties, and management of ethnic relations.[184] In its engagement, Indonesia has made sure it does not position itself as "superior" in relation to Myanmar and stressed that Myanmar has ownership in the peace process.
- Indonesia has also helped conduct election monitoring in Myanmar, having sent monitors to observe elections in 2010 and 2015.[185] During the 2014 elections, the Asia Foundation sponsored a tour for a delegation from Myanmar's Union Election Commission (UEC) to visit Indonesia. This included a meeting with the chair and commissioners of the Indonesian National Election Commission, the local election commission in Yogyakarta, and the NGO Perludem. The delegation also met with Google's Jakarta office (on how it

engaged Indonesia's voters and provided access to 2014 elections information using online services), the Institute for Inclusion and Advocacy of Persons with Disabilities, and Solidaritas Perempuan, which focuses on women's rights in Indonesia.[186] Lastly, Indonesia has invited outside observers to monitor its own elections in several instances, including most recently the 2019 general election.[187]

- Due to the recent political crisis in Myanmar, President Jokowi and Malaysian prime minister Muhyiddin Yassin have instructed their top diplomats to initiate a regional meeting to respond to developments. To realize the vision of an ASEAN Community, the president said it was important for Myanmar to respect the principles enshrined in the ASEAN Charter, especially rule of law, good governance, democracy, human rights, and constitutional government.[188]

- Given that Indonesia has the world's largest Muslim community, it has sought to address the concerns and pressures from its Muslim constituents to end violence and discrimination against the Rohingya ethnic group. Until recently, Indonesia would provide technical assistance to Myanmar in general, while simultaneously providing technical assistance to Rohingya communities in Rakhine. In doing so, Indonesia sought to alleviate pressures on the Rohingya while mollifying the Myanmar government. Muhammadiyah, one of the largest religious-based NGOs in Indonesia, has collaborated with other NGOs in the region, including one local NGO in Myanmar, to explore possible areas of peacebuilding to deal with the Rohingya issue.[189]

Multilateral Support: Indonesia's Efforts in ASEAN

Indonesia has been a major proponent of advocating for democracy and human rights within ASEAN. In 2003, the Indonesian government pushed to include a human rights dimension in the ASEAN Security Community concept in the Bali Concord II declaration. In 2007, Indonesia was the first to push ASEAN to adopt democratic values as part of its charter. It then lobbied for an ASEAN Intergovernmental Commission on Human Rights, and an ASEAN Human Rights Declaration. The former was established in 2009, and the later was signed in 2012. Indonesia has since used ASEAN as a vehicle for nurturing its regional leadership and promoting democracy in the region through "sharing" its own democratization experience and challenges.[190]

NONGOVERNMENTAL ACTOR INVOLVED IN DEMOCRACY SUPPORT: THE HABIBIE CENTER

The Habibie Center was founded by former president Bacharuddin Jusuf Habibie and his family as an independent, nongovernmental, and nonprofit organization with a vision to advance modernization and democratization efforts in Indonesia based on morality, cultural integrity, and religious values.[191] It does so largely through crafting articles and reports on democracy-related issues in the region, convening public events at the Track 2 and 1.5 levels, and occasionally privately mediating conflicts and facilitating peacebuilding.

The main vehicle through which the Habibie Center supports democracy beyond its borders is through its ASEAN Studies Program. The center releases reports on all aspects of democracy support and promotion in the region, including human rights, media, civil society, and governance. The center also holds events that largely focus on sharing Indonesia's best practices and pitfalls in relation to its own democratization.[192] These events are more often Track 2 and therefore support a network of nonprofits, academics, think tanks, and other sub-government actors. The center's efforts in this regard are best thought of as complementing government efforts, such as the Track 1 BDF.

The Habibie Center also takes part in private dialogues and sometimes even peacebuilding activities. It had a role in convening stakeholders in Myanmar's peacebuilding process in the 2010s.

OPPORTUNITIES FOR DEMOCRATIC PARTNERSHIP

1. **Indonesia should prioritize the "three Ts" in its support for democracy in the region: technical cooperation, "trilateralization," and transition.** Indonesia's value as a supporter of democracy is its leadership by example as a Southeast Asian Islamic nation. In the past, it has greatly benefited from third-party collaboration on democracy with countries such as Australia, Japan, the United Kingdom, and Germany, as they can provide significant amounts of ODA and expertise. In addition, Indonesia's

support has historically been most impactful when technical in nature, such as funding for training, and targeted at countries that are in transition, such as Timor-Leste. Indonesia should therefore coordinate with the United States, Japan, and others to support technical assistance in countries that are making the transition toward democracy, for example, through workshops and seminars on democracy and rule of law.

2. **Indonesia should revive the focus on democracy in its foreign policy strategy.** Indonesia was able to make positive headway in the 2000s, especially with more direct democracy support efforts starting in 2010. However, since 2015, democracy support has largely reverted to development efforts without an explicit focus on democracy. Indonesia enhanced its diplomatic and strategic weight by utilizing its convening power to shape regional discourse on democracy through ASEAN, and a revival of those efforts would prove critical in the face of democratic backsliding across the region.

3. **Indonesia should assume a leadership role in the United States' Summit for Democracy by focusing on its unique position as the world's third-largest democracy and a Muslim-majority country.** Indonesia has often stressed that democratic values and Islam are complementary rather than incompatible. Given that the Biden administration is focused on including a diverse array of countries in the democracy summit, Indonesia should work with the United States to convene a constellation of dialogues on Southeast Asia's experience with democracy.

SOUTH KOREA
"Important Middle Power"

OVERVIEW

South Korean discussions of democracy and human rights promotion began in the 1990s with South Korea's interest in global leadership diplomacy and its desire to play a more deliberate and dynamic role on the international stage commensurate with its economic success. Despite this effort in the 1990s, democracy has not featured prominently in South Korea's ODA policy and overall foreign policy strategy. As a result, South Korea's approach to ODA has been largely technocratic in nature. Recognizing this gap, in 2018, South Korea committed to enhancing its democracy-related ODA through the Korea International Cooperation Agency's (KOICA) new basic plan for implementation centered on peace, justice, and governance. Importantly, under the new plan, KOICA will apply a bottom-up, grassroots approach to its aid and focus more explicitly on democracy support. Following this shift, South Korea has been more active in partnering with local NGOs and the private sector and has also increased its cooperation on democracy support multilaterally and bilaterally with the United States. South Korea's Ministry of Foreign Affairs (MOFA) oversees the formulation and implementation of grant aid policies, and KOICA is the executive agency for ODA, providing grants and implementing development projects. Other than the government, civil society groups in South Korea are also active in democracy support across the region, such as the Asia Democracy Research Network, the Jeju Forum for Peace and Prosperity, and the Asia Democracy Network.[193]

KOICA directs a large amount of its ODA toward the Asia-Pacific. In 2018, 42 percent of KOICA's total annual assistance (about KRW 134.4 billion or $114 million) went toward 16 partner countries in the Asia-Pacific region.[194] Moreover, almost half of KOICA's priority partner countries are within the Asia-Pacific region.[195] A priority sector for KOICA ODA activities is "governance," specifically in public administration; the overall objective is to increase the accountability, inclusiveness, and effectiveness of institutions for sustainable development. In 2018, approximately 22.6 percent of total annual assistance to Asia (about KRW 29.5 billion or $25 million) was used to support projects in the "public administration" sector. Another priority sector for KOICA is "human rights," with the purpose of establishing an inclusive and peaceful society.

BACKGROUND AND RECENT TRENDS

South Korea's transition to democracy began after the June Uprising democratic demonstrations in 1987, resulting in the election of Kim Young-sam as president in 1992. Economic development and increased social mobilization raised popular demands for political participation, providing the economic and social foundation for democracy. Following the election, the Kim Young-sam administration (1993–1998) laid some of the groundwork for emphasizing democracy promotion in South Korea's foreign policy. In 1993, then foreign minister Han Sung-joo announced South Korea's "New Diplomacy," signaling its willingness to work with other nations to resolve global issues related to international peace and security. These policies also emphasized that in an era of globalization, South Korean diplomacy must also focus on the promotion of universal values such as freedom, justice, peace, and welfare.[196] At the May 1994 ASEAN Regional Forum Senior Officials' Meeting, the Kim Young-sam administration also introduced the *Republic of Korea's Paper on Northeast Asia Security Cooperation*, a report advocating for multilateral security cooperation in Northeast Asia on the basis of democracy and respect for human dignity, among other principles.[197]

Despite this positive trend toward democracy promotion in the 1990s and South Korea's unique experiences with democratization, democracy does not feature prominently in the country's ODA policy. South Korea's overall strategy adheres more closely to principles of noninterference in recipient countries' internal affairs. As a result, South Korea's approach to ODA has so far been largely technocratic in nature, focusing mainly on building strong and capable institutions that are not necessarily democratic.[198] This technocratic model of development, which supports the need for economic development followed by a process of democratization, also mirrors South Korea's own experiences.[199] Since its establishment in 1991, KOICA has dedicated only about 20 percent of its overall ODA to what it calls the "Public Administration" sector.[200]

Recognizing this gap in its democracy-related ODA, South Korea established a basic plan for implementation in May 2018 that centers on peace, justice (human rights), and governance (democracy). Specifically, KOICA declared that projects beginning in 2020 will be expanded from public administration to overall governance to better realize universal values of gender equality, peace, democracy, and human rights.[201] Under this new basic plan, KOICA will also apply both a top-down approach that strengthens capabilities of partner countries and a bottom-up approach that strengthens the capabilities of individuals and civil society. This new basic plan is notable for its more explicit focus on promoting democracy, as opposed to governance and public administration more generally. It also reflects a move away from "scattered, one-off projects focusing on improving the efficiency of the executive arm of the partner country's government" to a more deliberate grassroots-centered participatory approach to projects.[202] For example, KOICA is enhancing cooperation with local NGOs through the "Peace Action Coalition for Everyone" (PEACE) Initiative and focusing on increasing public-private partnerships (see page 29).

KOICA identifies "priority partner countries" for its ODA disbursements to allow the government to more effectively concentrate its resources. Eleven of its 24 priority partner countries are in Asia, and KOICA's assistance to these 11 countries in 2018 amounted to 92.3 percent of its total assistance for the region that year.[203] Within Asia, the majority of South Korea's ODA is concentrated in Southeast Asia. KOICA also identifies "priority sectors" for its ODA activities, such as governance, with an overall objective to increase the accountability, inclusiveness, and effectiveness of institutions for sustainable development.[204] Strategic objectives include enhanced administrative service, accountability of the political administrative system, and an inclusive legal system. Another priority sector is human rights, with an overall objective of establishing an inclusive and peaceful society.[205] Strategic objectives include protecting the human rights of socially marginalized people and facilitating their access to justice, encouraging local resident–led peace, and establishing transparent, responsible, and inclusive governance systems.

GOVERNMENT SUPPORT FOR DEMOCRACY-RELATED INITIATIVES

Public Administration and Good Governance

As mentioned above, nearly half of KOICA's total annual assistance budget went toward 16 Asia-Pacific partner countries, and over 20 percent of this assistance was used to support projects in the "Public Administration" sector. Examples include:

- The Digital Partnership for Inclusive Development project between South Korea and ASEAN aims to close the inequality gap within ASEAN through digital connectivity, including through improving public information services such as civil complaint processing and information on law. Key beneficiaries are Cambodia, Laos, Myanmar, Vietnam, Indonesia, and the Philippines.[206]

- South Korea's implementation plan for its development assistance to Vietnam includes training and capacity building of judges to contribute to an independent judicial system in Vietnam. Its capacity-building projects target inspection agencies such as the Supreme People's Prosecutor of Vietnam, the Government Inspectorate, and the State Audit Office of Vietnam.[207] In 2018, KOICA provided about KRW 31.6 billion (approximately $26.8 million) for its country partnership projects with Vietnam to help Vietnam carry out its national development goals. Included among the various focus areas was the enhancement of public sector capacity building.[208] Another program KOICA has implemented in Vietnam is the Establishment of Effective, Responsible and Transparent Governance and Institutions.[209] Lastly, from 2019 to 2023, KOICA committed $12 million to the Increased Transparency in Legal Procedures and Quality of Court Rulings in Vietnam project.[210]

- South Korea's stated vision for development assistance to Myanmar includes "supporting the efforts of the Government of Myanmar in strengthening democracy, good governance, rule of law, national reconciliation, and human rights."[211] Accordingly, KOICA's implementation strategies for its ODA to Myanmar include contributing to the development of a legal information system to strengthen the rule of law in Myanmar and helping to build an e-government system to increase government transparency.[212] In 2018, KOICA provided about KRW 16.3 billion (approximately $13.8 million) for its country partnership projects with Myanmar to help fulfill Myanmar's national development goals. Strengthening public administration and governance was included as one of the focus areas.[213] From 2015 to 2019, South Korea provided $3.65 million to provide training for professionals in the legislative system under the Project for the Establishment of Law Information System.[214] Since 2015, KOICA has helped establish a legislation database, launched local workshops, and provided training for Myanmar's Justice Department officials in South Korea.

- In 2018, KOICA provided about KRW 3.8 billion (approximately $3.2 million) for its country partnership projects with Indonesia to help Indonesia fulfill its national development tasks. KOICA's focus included strengthening Indonesia's capacities for governance and public administration.[215] Examples of projects include the Digital Partnership for Inclusive Development, the Participatory and Transparent Governance in Indonesia Project by UNDP, and the KOICA-UNDP Partnership for Capacity Development for an Integrated National Compliant Handling System in Indonesia.[216]

- In 2018, KOICA provided KRW 4.6 billion (approximately $3.9 million) for its country partnership projects with Mongolia. This funding helped promote the establishment of an efficient public administration system, including public services based on information and communications technology (ICT) to increase transparency and accountability for Mongolia's public services.[217] Examples of projects include the Improved Governance for Sustainable Development project and the project for the Establishment of E-court Service System for the Constitutional Court of Mongolia.[218]

- Other projects in South Asia include Enhancing Public Sector Accountability through Institutional Strengthening in Anti-Corruption and Decentralization in East Timor, the ICT-based Governance Reinforcement project in Nepal, the ICT-based Improvement of Laws and Institutions to Strengthen the Social Safety Net project in Bangladesh, and the Strengthened Democratic Institutions for Inclusive Development project in Sri Lanka.[219]

Women's Empowerment

- South Korea and the United States are cooperating to promote women's empowerment by leveraging the Providing Opportunities for Women's Economic Rise

(POWER) Initiative. The two countries are coordinating consultations with private sector entities in their respective nations to elevate the issue at corporate levels and build strategic partnerships with the public sector.

- In 2018, KOICA launched a new project in Vietnam titled Building a Model to Respond to Violence Against Women and Girls in Viet Nam. The project's objective is to strengthen Vietnam's national and institutional capacity to provide essential services for GBV survivors in response to violence against women and girls in Vietnam. This includes improving the infrastructure of social work centers to provide essential services for GBV survivors, such as counseling, support, and referral services. Most of the $2.5 million budget for the project comes from KOICA ODA.[220]

- Foreign Minister Kang Kyung-wha announced the launch of the Action with Women and Peace initiative on June 19, 2018, to increase the South Korean government's contributions to women, peace, and security.[221] The main objective of the initiative is to carry out development cooperation projects for victims of sexual violence to help eliminate sexual violence in conflict. The initiative also aims to "hold an international meeting on a regular basis to advance the international discussions on women, peace, and security."[222] To implement the initiative, the Foreign Ministry will also "establish close cooperative relations with relevant civil society and academia and devise measures to help experts in civil society grow into international experts and make contributions."[223]

Partnership with Civil Society, NGOs, and the Private Sector

KOICA has incrementally been increasing its work with NGOs and the private sector. In 2012, South Korea launched the Development Alliance Korea project to establish and coordinate public-private partnerships.[224] In 2016, KOICA announced that one of the key pillars in the South Korean government's Mid-Term Strategy for Development Cooperation (2016–2020) is "collaborative ODA." Under this principle, the government commits to diversifying partnerships with the private sector.[225] Following this announcement, KOICA provided about KRW 27.1 billion (approximately $23 million) to 119 public-private partnership projects in 2018 for grassroots-type projects funded by civic organizations, universities, and social enterprises.[226] Included among these public-private partnership projects were programs aimed at empowering developing countries' residents and creating global social values. Four out of the top five partner countries for public-private partnership projects were countries in the Asia-Pacific region (Vietnam, Mongolia, Cambodia, and Indonesia).

In 2019, to better promote the core values of the UN SDGs, KOICA also introduced the PEACE Initiative. The aim of this initiative is to establish an inclusive and peaceful society through strengthening capabilities of local residents. It targets strengthening the capabilities of local NGOs, grassroots citizens, and government policies and implementation. The project, which runs from 2020 to 2024, has a total budget of $300 million.[227] In January 2019, the South Korean government also established the "Basic Policy for Government-Civic Society Partnership for International Development Cooperation" to promote inclusive collaboration with South Korean and local civic groups overseas.[228]

A SAMPLE OF SOUTH KOREAN NONGOVERNMENTAL ACTORS INVOLVED IN DEMOCRACY SUPPORT

Asia Democracy Network

- The Asia Democracy Network (ADN) was launched in October 2013 by the Korea Democracy Foundation, the Korea Human Rights Foundation, and the East Asia Institute.[229] It gathers civil society actors from across Asia who are experts in the field of human rights and democracy and holds a regular forum for knowledge sharing and dialogue.[230]

- The ADN's vision is to "promote and advance democratization and democratic governance at all levels of society through effective solidarity and cooperation among civil society organizations and democracy advocates in Asia."[231] The ADN is a regional network that includes a diverse pool of civil society actors, which allows it to leverage expert knowledge and perspectives in its work, especially in its youth programming.[232] This is especially the case for its flagship initiatives: the annual youth assembly and the annual youth leadership program.[233] The ADN also offers online, offline, and hybrid democracy education through its educational program, the Asia Democracy Academy.[234]

- The ADN has partnered with the Community of Democracies Permanent Secretariat to host an Asia regional Democracy Forum every year since 2018. The forum's objective is to discuss the UN SDGs—especially Goal 16, which aims to "promote peaceful and inclusive societies for sustainable development, provide access to justice for all and build effective, accountable and inclusive institutions at all levels."[235]

Asia Democracy Research Network

- Launched in 2013, the Asia Democracy Research Network (ADRN) conducts research related to democratic governance and human rights promotion in Asia. Its secretariat is the East Asia Institute, which is responsible for supporting the ADRN, managing its research, and dealing with related activities of ADRN members. The ADRN currently operates in 14 Asian countries and includes 23 major think tanks.[236]

- In supporting democracy-related research and collaboration, the ADRN is an important player within South Korea's nonprofit sector for promoting democracy throughout the region. Specifically, the ADRN organizes workshops in its various member countries and online, publishes democracy-related research, and engages with other networks in this field, such as the East Asia Institute's Myanmar Program and the U.S. National Endowment for Democracy.[237]

Jeju Forum for Peace and Prosperity

- The Jeju Forum for Peace and Prosperity was launched in 2001 and was held biennially until 2011, after which it became an annual event. It is a regional multilateral dialogue which aims to promote peace and prosperity in Asia with support from the South Korean MOFA. Its secretariat is located on Jeju Island. Over 70 nations participate in the forum, with around 5,500 participants and 50 partner organizations. The forum is co-hosted by the International Peace Foundation and the East Asia Foundation. Past themes include "Sustainable Peace, Inclusive Prosperity" (2021), "Reinventing Multilateral Cooperation: Pandemic and Humane Security" (2020), and "Asia Towards Resilient Peace: Cooperation and Integration" (2019).[238]

OPPORTUNITIES FOR DEMOCRATIC PARTNERSHIP

1. **Collaborate closely with Quad countries on democracy efforts.** While South Korea is not a formal Quad member, it should still consider engaging in some "Quad+" activities centered around the common goal of democracy support. Increasing multilateral cooperation on democracy support efforts is an important tool to combat democratic backsliding in the region. This will send a strong signal that regional democracies are aligned on the importance of democratic norms and values in their foreign policies and can help combine resources to support regional governments and NGOs more effectively.

2. **Enhance cooperation with regional partners on women's empowerment.** South Korea and the United States are already doing meaningful work on gender equality and women's empowerment through efforts such as the POWER initiative, and Japan, South Korea, and the United States have recently begun cooperating at the trilateral level through the U.S.-Japan-ROK Women's Empowerment Trilateral Forum.[239] South Korea should expand this cooperation and form working groups on women's empowerment with other regional partners that are active in this area, such as Australia, and host seminars or conferences to involve diverse regional actors and NGOs.

3. **Create a digital technology initiative focused on building and promoting democratic norms.** South Korea is currently stressing a digital component in its democracy support work on good governance, especially through capacity-building efforts with ASEAN. South Korean assistance addresses overall digital connectivity as well as how technology is used in the judicial system and in other democratic processes. Given the importance of democratic norm building for these new digital technologies, South Korea is in a great position to bring regional partners together and discuss how technology should be used to enhance democratic values rather than undermine them.

TAIWAN

"Democracy Diplomat"

OVERVIEW

Taiwan's foreign aid strategy focuses mainly on the Indo-Pacific region, especially in the Pacific Islands. Most Taiwanese aid contributes indirectly to the promotion of democratic norms by focusing on technological, economic, and agricultural assistance and capacity building; however, the Taiwan Foundation for Democracy (TFD), founded in 2003 with support from Taiwan's Ministry of Foreign Affairs (MOFA), provides aid explicitly in support of democracy.

TFD projects include initiatives supporting a free press, women's empowerment, good governance, and judicial reform. The TFD also hosts the annual East Asia Democracy Forum, which convenes members of civil society from across Asia to promote and consolidate democratic development in the region. In 2018, Taiwan supplied $302 million in foreign aid.[240] By comparison, the TFD provided roughly $634,000 in international grants specifically related to democracy support in 2018.[241]

BACKGROUND AND RECENT TRENDS

Taiwan provides a significant amount of financial assistance to developing countries. Aid initiatives focus mainly on technological, economic, and agricultural capacity building in the Pacific Islands and Central America. Taiwan's ODA is not very transparent, as it does not break down its expenditures by type, so only limited information about the ratio of grants to loans is available.[242] Taiwan's foreign aid for capacity building is an indirect form of democracy support, as it prepares recipient countries for the socioeconomic conditions that facilitate democratic governance.

Direct support for democracy is provided by the TFD with funding from Taiwan's Ministry of Foreign Affairs. The TFD is a nonprofit, nonpartisan organization with board members representing political parties, government, academia, NGOs, and the business sector.[243] It provides aid to foreign countries and domestic organizations expressly for the purpose of bolstering democratic institutions and principles such as good governance and the rule of law. It provides grants to support the freedom of the press, women's empowerment, and judicial systems.

The TFD also hosts the annual East Asia Democracy Forum (EADF), launched in 2014, to convene members of civil society from across Asia to promote and consolidate democratic development in the region.[244] Since its founding, the EADF has been holding annual events, including steering committee meetings, international conferences, and workshops in Asia. Recent themes include preventing democratic backsliding (2018) and combating disinformation (2019).[245] In 2018, the EADF specifically focused on the emergence of an "alternative model" of governance offered by authoritarian regimes and discussed how democracies should work together to combat disinformation and develop counter-narratives to authoritarian models.[246] In 2019, the EADF continued this theme by discussing ways for government, civil society, and the private sector to deal with pressure from authoritarian regimes' influence tactics and disinformation.[247] In 2020, the EADF released a statement highlighting the challenges facing democracy due to the Covid-19 pandemic in Asia, emphasizing the importance of democratic values and institutions during this time.[248]

TFD SUPPORT FOR DEMOCRACY-RELATED INITIATIVES

Media and Free Press

- TFD International Grants in 2019 for media and the free press included a project in Indonesia, COCONET 2: Asia-Pacific Digital Rights Camp, organized by the Engage Media Collective. Another project was

Table 2: TFD International Grants 2019 (in $NT)

FOCUS AREA	GRANTS	AMOUNT GRANTED	SHARE OF YEARLY TOTAL
Global Democracy Movement	10	$1,688,377	9.5%
Asia Regional Democracy Movement	9	$4,857,588	27.3%
China Human Rights	19	$2,856,319	16.0%
Taiwan Studies	11	$1,888,048	10.6%
Southeast Asia	20	$2,425,662	13.6%
South Asia	18	$1,749,800	9.8%
Northeast Asia	4	$724,838	4.1%
Think Tanks	4	$1,215,360	6.8%
Other	5	$409,992	2.3%
Total	**100**	**$17,815,984**	**100%**

Source: "International Grants in 2019," Taiwan Foundation for Democracy, n.d., http://www.tfd.org.tw/opencms/english/grants/international/International0018.html.

conducted in Thailand, the International Conference on Fake News and Electoral Democracy in Asia, organized by the Asia Centre.[249]

Women's Empowerment

- TFD international grants in 2019 for women's empowerment included a project in Indonesia, Women and Radicalism: Dialogue to Overcome Misunderstanding of the Radicalism Issue, organized by Yayasan PUPA; the Promotion of Human Rights and Access to Women's Rights at Grassroots Level project in Bangladesh; and the Strengthening Democracy through Enhancing Women's Political Participation in Local Body Elections project in Pakistan.[250]

Judicial System

- In 2019, TFD international grants for judicial system capacity building included a project in Nepal, titled Advancing Dalits' Human Rights and Access to Justice through Evidence-Based Advocacy.[251]

TECHNICAL SUPPORT, DEVELOPMENT ASSISTANCE, AND FOREIGN AID RELATED TO CIVIL SOCIETY

Aid to Pacific Island Countries

Between 2006 and 2011, Taiwan provided $271 million in aid to Pacific Island countries, or about $237 per capita. Types of aid included technical support to Fiji, computer donations to Papua New Guinea, and medical assistance funding to the whole region. Taiwanese aid has focused on providing technical assistance, especially in agriculture and health, as well as on providing government scholarships. Taiwan also supports small-to-medium-sized infrastructure projects, such as a solar power plant in Nauru.[252]

Taiwan also supports people-to-people links. For example, in 2013, the East-West Center in Hawaii launched a five-year Pacific Islands Leadership Program, which featured "regional analysis of emerging issues in Oceania" and "experiential leadership learning and a commitment to practical action." The program, which has now been extended to 2023, aims to build connections between regional leaders "dedicated to shaping the future prosperity of the Pacific region." The program had garnered participation from a total of 144 Pacific youth leaders by 2018 and is funded by Taiwan's Institute of Diplomacy and International Affairs within MOFA.[253]

The Ministry of Foreign Affairs of Taiwan

In 2018, Taiwan gave $302 million in foreign aid, focused on its diplomatic allies and friendly countries. Much of this aid was related to eradicating poverty; providing energy, technology, and infrastructure support; and sharing agricultural resources and best practices. There are no explicit mentions of foreign aid specifically targeted toward democracy support activities such as press freedom, election reform, or human rights. However, technical aid can indirectly benefit the building blocks of democracy. Moreover, Taiwan is implementing development cooperation projects in line with the SDGs, which encourage countries to focus on development, peace, and human rights.[254]

Taiwan's MOFA also coordinates with the United States in discussions on democratic governance in the region. The American Institute in Taiwan, in cooperation with Taiwan's MOFA and the Bureau of Democracy, Human Rights, and Labor of the U.S. Department of State, began consultations in 2019 on how to share Taiwan's good governance experience with other countries in the region.[255] In September and October 2020, they held the second annual U.S.-Taiwan Consultations on Democratic Governance in the Indo-Pacific to "advance joint projects to strengthen democratic institutions and address pressing governance challenges."[256] Project areas include combating disinformation and securing joint funding for anti-corruption, open government, democracy, and human rights.[257] U.S.-Taiwan coordination on these initiatives seeks to demonstrate the centrality of democratic values in upholding a free and open Indo-Pacific region.[258]

- The U.S.-Taiwan Tech Challenge on Countering Disinformation and Propaganda initiative brings together companies from the United States, Taiwan, Israel, and Australia to explore ways to build democratic resiliency against disinformation through technology. The U.S. Department of State's Global Engagement Center awarded $250,000 to two participants to advance the development of their proposed technologies to combat disinformation and propaganda online.[259]

International Cooperation and Development Fund

The International Cooperation and Development Fund is a Taiwanese NGO that facilitates international development projects around the world. Areas of focus include the environment, public health and medicine, agriculture, education, and ICT. The fund's goals seem to have shifted away from democracy promotion and human rights since 2001, but this type of indirect support still helps to build up civil society in target countries. Current projects related to democracy promotion include the Women and Youth Entrepreneurs and Micro, Small and Medium Enterprises (MSMEs) Re-lending Project in Palau.[260]

OPPORTUNITIES FOR DEMOCRATIC PARTNERSHIP

1. **Increase democracy support to Pacific Island countries.** Taiwan devotes a large portion of its foreign aid to Pacific Island countries for technical assistance and infrastructure development projects. Taiwan should further its efforts to demonstrate the importance of capacity building as a foundation for democratic governance in the Pacific Islands to supplement similar efforts by other regional actors.

2. **Support the development of the legal and judicial sectors in developing countries.** Other donors in the region, such as Japan, have developed expertise in this field and provide development aid for legal training such as seminars on drafting civil codes. Taiwan should consider allocating resources to this cause and further its commitment to bolstering the institutional foundations of democracy in the region.

ALPHA CASE

The United States

The United States is the global leader in ODA and support for democracy, with over $2 billion allocated annually over the past decade for democracy promotion activities.[261] Over the past few years, the U.S. Agency for International Development (USAID) budget has been fairly constant for programs related to democracy, human rights, and governance.[262] While the Trump administration proposed cuts to foreign aid, this was met with opposition in Congress, reflecting bipartisan consensus on the importance of assistance for democratic governance as a means of supporting U.S. foreign policy objectives, advancing U.S. security, and promoting U.S. values and economic interests.[263] The Biden administration has stressed the importance of support for democracy as part of its foreign policy strategy, as exemplified by an FY 2022 $2.8 billion budget request for foreign assistance funding for democracy, human rights, and governance programming.[264] The Biden administration is also emphasizing the threats to democracy posed by Chinese and Russian authoritarianism and plans to assume a leadership role in championing democratic values through the Summit for Democracy and other efforts. Support for democracy could feature more prominently in the context of strategic competition with China and Russia and the need to defend the rules-based international order.

USAID and the U.S. Department of State are the main government actors funding democracy support initiatives abroad.[265] USAID generally designs and manages assistance programs and partners with NGOs for implementation, and activities are often integrated into the broader development strategies of recipient countries. Department of State democracy assistance focuses more on short-term emergency assistance. The Bureau of Democracy, Human Rights, and Labor serves as a grant-making entity and provides funds to U.S. nonprofits involved in promoting democracy and human rights. Over the past decade, good governance, the rule of law, and human rights have emerged as the highest-funded subcategories of USAID democracy promotion assistance.[266]

The United States is active in Asia. In 2020, democracy assistance was concentrated largely in Southeast Asia and South Asia, with Myanmar, Bangladesh, Cambodia, the Philippines, Vietnam, and Nepal standing out as key recipients. U.S. democracy-related ODA supports recipient governments, NGOs and civil society, public-private partnerships, and multilateral organizations. In 2020, $2.4 billion was appropriated for democracy, human rights, and governance, of which $261 million went to Central Asia, South Asia, East Asia, and Southeast Asia. An additional $124.7 million was appropriated for Afghanistan and Pakistan.[267] Afghanistan has received the most funding for democracy support in recent years, though future funding levels are uncertain in the wake of the U.S. withdrawal.

The United States is also unique in that NGOs and the private sector, as well as the government, are involved in promoting democracy support. U.S. democracy-related nonprofit organizations (NPOs) and NGOs such as the National Endowment for Democracy, International Republican Institute, and National Democratic Institute are involved in numerous activities involving operational planning, research and policy advice, and financial assistance to democratic institutions and organizations.[268] The private sector plays a role in democracy support through its commitment to labor rights, transparency, anti-corruption, and governance and by incorporating human rights into their overseas operations.

ABOUT THE AUTHORS

Michael Jonathan Green is senior vice president for Asia and Japan Chair at the Center for Strategic and International Studies (CSIS) and director of Asian Studies at the Edmund A. Walsh School of Foreign Service at Georgetown University. He served on the staff of the National Security Council (NSC) from 2001 through 2005, first as director for Asian affairs with responsibility for Japan, Korea, Australia, and New Zealand, and then as special assistant to the president for national security affairs and senior director for Asia, with responsibility for East Asia and South Asia. Before joining the NSC staff, he was a senior fellow for East Asian security at the Council on Foreign Relations, director of the Edwin O. Reischauer Center and the Foreign Policy Institute and assistant professor at the School of Advanced International Studies at Johns Hopkins University, research staff member at the Institute for Defense Analyses, and senior adviser on Asia in the Office of the Secretary of Defense. He also worked in Japan on the staff of a member of the National Diet.

Nicholas Szechenyi is deputy director of the Japan Chair at the Center for Strategic and International Studies (CSIS) where he is also a senior fellow. His research focuses on U.S.-Japan relations and U.S.-East Asia relations. Prior to joining CSIS in 2005, he was a news producer for Fuji Television in Washington, D.C., where he covered U.S. policy in Asia and domestic politics. He holds an MA in international economics and Japan studies from the Johns Hopkins University School of Advanced International Studies and a BA in Asian studies from Connecticut College.

Hannah Fodale is an associate fellow with the Japan Chair at the Center for Strategic and International Studies (CSIS), where she focuses on projects involving U.S.-Japan relations and security in the Indo-Pacific region. She is also the editor of the Debating Japan newsletter and producer of the Asia Chessboard podcast. Prior to joining CSIS, she spent time working for the U.S. Department of State in Okinawa, Japan. She holds an MA in security studies and a BS in foreign service from the School of Foreign Service at Georgetown University.

ANNEX: A CATALOGUE OF REGIONAL NETWORKS AND INSTITUTIONS

Below is an illustrative list of regional and global networks and institutions that the United States could potentially leverage to collaborate with like-minded allies and partners on democracy support.

Regional Networks

BILATERAL RELATIONSHIPS

U.S.-Japan Alliance

The United States and Japan are natural partners for cooperating on democracy support assistance. Specifically, U.S.-Japan strategic alignment under the Free and Open Indo-Pacific (FOIP) vision presents numerous opportunities for collaboration in supporting democratic rules and norms in the economic, maritime, and diplomatic arenas.[269] The Japan-U.S. Strategic Energy Partnership, Japan-U.S. Strategic Digital Economy Partnership, and Japan-U.S. Mekong Power Partnership are all examples of rule-making and standard-setting initiatives based on openness and transparency designed to help realize a free and open Indo-Pacific.[270]

U.S.-ROK Alliance

The United States and South Korea (Republic of Korea or ROK) are also cooperating on democracy support in the region. The U.S. FOIP Strategy and ROK New Southern Policy (NSP) represent a convergence in views on the importance of democratic rules and norms based on the principles of openness, inclusiveness, transparency, respect for international norms, and ASEAN centrality. The NSP is South Korea's core diplomatic initiative aimed at realizing mutual prosperity and peace in East Asia and the world by elevating relations with ASEAN member states and India. It is based on the three pillars of people, prosperity, and peace. The "people" pillar of the NSP overlaps with FOIP's emphasis on good governance and support for civil society.[271] The 2019 memorandum of understanding (MOU) signed by USAID and South Korea's MOFA, KOICA-USAID collaboration, and U.S.-ROK collaboration on Asia EDGE exemplify ongoing alliance coordination in the region to strengthen and promote democratic and responsive governments.[272] The United States is also specifically coordinating with South Korea on women's empowerment by leveraging the Providing Opportunities for Women's Economic Rise (POWER) initiative.[273] This State Department initiative promotes women's economic empowerment in a global context through collaboration with the private sector.[274] The May 2021 U.S.-ROK joint statement also mentions a shared vision for support of democratic norms, human rights, and the rule of law in the region; a commitment to democratic values and the promotion of human rights; and collaboration on women's empowerment and anti-corruption initiatives.[275]

U.S.-Australia Alliance

In July 2020, USAID and DFAT signed an MOU on international development cooperation that recognizes goals and objectives related to democracy support. These include:

- "advancing an open, inclusive, prosperous, and secure Indo-Pacific region";
- "supporting development that promotes effective and accountable governance, human rights and dignity";

- "working with the multilateral system to strengthen the rules-based order and ensure global institutions are fit for purpose to address current challenges, accountable to their Member States, free from undue influence and politicization, and focused appropriately on the Indo-Pacific region"; and

- "recognizing and sharing different development skills, including the planning and delivery of development-assistance and humanitarian programs, and leveraging the comparative advantage of each Participant to assist governments, civil society, faith-based organizations, and the private sector in partner countries to support national resilience, prosperity, and stability."[276]

Areas of cooperation focus on institution building and civil society promotion, economic governance, women's empowerment, and gender equality.[277] In addition, the recent 2021 joint statement on Australia-U.S. Ministerial Consultations includes a section on democratic values and multilateralism and mentions closer cooperation on democratic resilience, human rights, and strengthening the rules-based international order.[278]

U.S.-India Partnership
The United States and India have coordinated democracy support activities in the past, including the establishment of the Community of Democracies in 2000, efforts to set up a United Nations Democracy Caucus in 2004, and the launch of a U.S.-India Global Democracy Initiative in 2005.[279] However, there is no formal agreement on democracy promotion between the two countries.[280] Coordination through the Quad remains an important avenue for the United States and India to jointly pursue activities supporting a free and open Indo-Pacific region based on democratic norms and the rule of law.

Japan-India Special Strategic and Global Partnership
Joint statements between Japan and India consistently point to shared values of democracy and the rule of law, but cooperation explicitly focused on democracy support or promotion is largely absent. India's Act East policy aligns with Japan's FOIP and has helped produce such initiatives as the Asia-Africa Growth Corridor, which is founded on core values of democracy, peace, rule of law, tolerance, and respect for the environment in realizing pluralistic and inclusive growth of the region.[281]

India-Australia Comprehensive Strategic Partnership
The India-Australia Comprehensive Strategic Partnership is based on mutual understanding, trust, common interests, and the shared values of democracy and rule of law. According to the joint statement signed by both Australia and India, "Both countries share the vision of an open, free, rules-based Indo-Pacific region supported by inclusive global and regional institutions that promote prosperous, stable, and sovereign states based on shared interests."[282] Additionally, India and Australia have confirmed their shared commitment to support the "freedom of navigation, overflight, and peaceful and cooperative use of the seas by adherence of all nations to international law including the United Nations Convention on the Law of the Sea (UNCLOS) and peaceful resolution of disputes rather than through unilateral or coercive actions."[283] In addition to cooperation in the maritime domain, "Both sides share a commitment to supporting a strong and resilient regional architecture with ASEAN at its center."[284] At the June 2020 India-Australia Virtual Summit, the Indian Department of Administrative Reforms and Public Grievances and the Australian Public Service Commission signed an MOU on cooperation in the field of public administration and governance reforms. The areas of cooperation under the MOU include "promoting transparency and accountability in

delivery of public services," "building effective service delivery in the public service," "recruitment and promotion in the public service," "training and capacity building of the public service," and "public sector management and reform."[285] Preliminary discussions are ongoing to implement the MOU.[286]

Japan-Australia Special Strategic Partnership
In 2016, Japan and Australia agreed to a "Strategy for Cooperation in the Pacific" based on their common values and strategic interests, including democracy, human rights, rule of law, open markets, and free trade, to help the Pacific region secure a peaceful and prosperous future. The strategy aims to support Pacific Island countries' efforts to "strengthen economic prosperity, peace, and stability in the region through effective governance, economic growth and sustainable development, security and defense cooperation, and diplomatic initiatives."[287] Both countries pledged to work closely together with multilateral organizations active in the region, such as the World Bank, the Asian Development Bank, and the UNDP.[288] Recent 2021 summit meetings mention further cooperation between Japan and Australia toward realizing a "Free and Open Indo-Pacific."[289]

U.S.-Taiwan Relationship
The American Institute in Taiwan, in cooperation with Taiwan's Ministry of Foreign Affairs and the Bureau of Democracy, Human Rights, and Labor of the U.S. Department of State, convened the second annual U.S.-Taiwan Consultations on Democratic Governance in the Indo-Pacific Region in September and October 2020 to advance joint projects to strengthen democratic institutions and address pressing governance challenges. Project areas include combating disinformation and joint funding for anti-corruption, open government, democracy, and human rights. U.S.-Taiwan coordination on these initiatives seeks to demonstrate the centrality of democratic values in upholding a free and open Indo-Pacific region.[290]

TRILATERAL NETWORKS

U.S.-Japan-Australia
The United States, Japan, and Australia coordinate trilaterally on quality infrastructure through the Trilateral Infrastructure Partnership, which was established by an MOU in November 2018. The partnership furthers the three countries' shared commitment to "promote an Indo-Pacific region that is free, open, inclusive, prosperous, and secure" through support for infrastructure projects that address the basic needs of the region and adhere to international standards and principles.[291] While these initiatives do not directly support democracy, they support key democratic themes such as openness and transparency. The United States, Japan, and Australia also support democracy indirectly through the Blue Dot Network (BDN). The BDN complements Japan's Expanded Partnership for Quality Infrastructure, the Trilateral Partnership for Infrastructure Investment in the Indo-Pacific, and FOIP principles and supports a strategy to ensure the adoption of global standards for quality infrastructure.[292] The BDN builds upon the G20 Summit principles from Buenos Aires and Osaka and supports the goals of East Asia Summit leaders.[293]

Australia-Japan-India
Australia, Japan, and India hold trilateral dialogues centered around maritime security and freedom of navigation. The first trilateral dialogue was held in 2015 and since then the trilateral relationship has emerged as an important "minilateral" grouping in the

region. The Australia-Japan-India Supply Chain Resilience Initiative, which launched after the 2020 Trilateral Dialogue, is an indicator of a more action-oriented agenda that the countries could pursue in the coming years.[294] While no explicitly democracy-related work has been proposed by the grouping, initiatives thus far complement FOIP principles and have the potential to advance democratic norms and rules.

Australia, Japan, and India also have overlapping Indo-Pacific outlooks. All three countries share a desire for rules-based regional multilateralism and harbor a common concern regarding the future role of a more assertive China in the region, though they still try to make sure their Indo-Pacific outlooks are open and inclusive. Defending freedom of navigation and rule of law has been a constant feature of the three countries' Indo-Pacific strategies, and the three governments consistently state an intention to coordinate their regional diplomacy.[295]

U.S.-Japan-ROK

While the three countries share aspirations to preserve and promote democratic values in the region, trilateral cooperation has largely remained in the security field.[296] However, there is significant overlap between FOIP and the NSP related to support for democratic principles, human rights, and civil society. The three countries are also actively promoting women's empowerment through the U.S.-Japan-ROK Women's Empowerment Trilateral Forum. Launched in 2016, this forum brings together leaders and elected officials from government, business, and civil society to discuss ways in which the three countries can work together to promote women's political and economic participation around the world.[297] The second trilateral forum took place in October 2020, with a specific focus on expanding women's leadership and participation in science, technology, engineering, and math.[298]

MULTILATERAL NETWORKS

Japan-ASEAN Cooperative Partnership

During the 23rd Japan-ASEAN Summit Meeting in November 2020, Prime Minister Yoshihide Suga confirmed Japan's support for the ASEAN Outlook on the Indo-Pacific (AOIP) and stated that it has many fundamental commonalities with Japan's FOIP vision. He expressed that Japan wishes to cooperate in accordance with AOIP's priority areas, including maritime cooperation, connectivity, and the SDGs.[299] While there are no democracy-related examples included in Japan's cooperation projects on AOIP as of November 2020, technical cooperation in maritime security and in quality infrastructure has the possibility to help institutionalize democratic norms of transparency, rule of law, and good governance.[300]

U.S.-ASEAN Strategic Partnership

A 2020 factsheet from the U.S. Mission to ASEAN confirms that the U.S.-ASEAN strategic partnership is built on "shared principles (as outlined in the U.S. Indo-Pacific Strategy and AOIP), including ASEAN centrality, respect for sovereignty and rule of law, good governance, transparency, inclusivity, rules-based frameworks, and openness."[301] It outlines that "through the Billion Futures Initiative, the United States and ASEAN will unleash the full potential of their combined 1 billion people in civil society, government, academia, and the private sector, in line with the connectivity pillar of the AOIP."[302] The Plan of Action to Implement the ASEAN-United States Strategic Partnership (2021–2025) lists goals and objectives explicitly related to democracy, such as supporting ASEAN's efforts in promoting good governance and the rule of law, including through the sharing of experiences and best practices; supporting ASEAN member states in anti-corruption efforts through the implementation of the United Nations Convention Against Corruption and ASEAN Parties Against Corruption; and supporting the ASEAN Intergovernmental Commission on Human Rights through capacity-building activities.[303] There are also sections of objectives surrounding women's empowerment, gender equality, and capacity building for the civil service.[304] In August 2021, when Secretary of State Anthony Blinken attended the annual U.S.-ASEAN Foreign Ministers' Meeting, he also stressed the strategic partnership for the Indo-Pacific and called on the Burmese military junta to restore democratic governance in Myanmar.[305]

The Quadrilateral Security Dialogue

Recent statements from the Quad have signaled that the minilateral may potentially take on a stronger approach to supporting democracy.[306] The joint statement from March 2021 confirmed support for democratic values, rule of law, and the strengthening of democratic resilience in the Indo-Pacific.[307] The September 2021 joint statement continued these sentiments, committing to supporting shared values of human rights and building democratic resilience in the Indo-Pacific.[308] The Quad has stated that restoring democracy in Myanmar and strengthening democratic resilience in the Indo-Pacific are priorities, and the Quad members' potential for success in Myanmar is notable.[309]

In 2019, the CSIS Alliances and American Leadership Project conducted an informal survey of elites in the four Quad countries as a "temperature check" on future possibilities for the grouping. Out of the three initiatives proposed to the respondents (one on a standing military task force, one on the standing up of a Quad Secretariat, and one on coordinating economic development and promoting human rights), support for Quad countries to coordinate economic and development assistance and promote human rights garnered the greatest support.[310]

Bali Democracy Forum

Elite support for the BDF, Indonesia's main vehicle for democracy promotion, has fallen in recent years. While former president Susilo Bambang Yudhoyono started the forum in 2008 and attended all forums from 2008 to 2014, his successor, President Jokowi, has only attended once. Ministerial-level officials and heads of state have also declined in attendance.[311] Nevertheless, the BDF still exists as a major convening body for democracies to discuss best practices and tackle common challenges. The 13th BDF was held in December of 2020 and addressed the theme of "Democracy and the Covid-19 Pandemic."[312]

South-South and Triangular Cooperation

South-South and Triangular Cooperation (SSTC) refers to a model of multilateral cooperation in which two or more "Global South" countries—decolonized developing countries—cooperate and coordinate in dealing with a "North" actor, usually a multilateral institution or developed country. This is to encourage equitable outcomes for developing countries and to ensure that developing countries are treated as true partners in international development.[313] SSTC is not primarily a vehicle for supporting democracy: it is a vehicle to ensure equitable terms for development through knowledge sharing. However, Indonesia uses SSTC to assist developing countries with negotiating project terms and capacity building, including for good governance and peacebuilding workshops and trainings.[314] The National Coordination Team of SSTC in Indonesia covers a wide range of countries in East and North Africa, Central Asia, and Southeast Asia.[315] Indonesia has also engaged with Afghanistan and Myanmar.

REGIONAL TRADE AGREEMENTS

CPTPP and RCEP

The rulemaking and norm-setting process for regional trade is most likely to be driven by two large trade agreements: the Comprehensive and Progressive Agreement for Trans-Pacific Partnership (CPTPP) and the Regional Comprehensive Economic Partnership (RCEP). The United States withdrew from CPTPP in 2017, but Japan and Australia have played instrumental roles in carrying forward a commitment to establishing regional rules and norms in the absence of U.S. leadership. The United States is not in RCEP but can rely on allies within RCEP, such as Japan, to promote values of openness, fairness, and transparency.

Regional Institutions

ASEAN REGIONAL FORUM

While the Asean Regional Forum (ARF) does not explicitly reference democracy promotion, in recent years it has focused on promoting democratic values such as fairness and the rule of law. Themes in the "Chairman's Statement of the 27th ARF" in 2020 included securing vaccine access, preserving supply chain connectivity, and maintaining and promoting peace, security, stability, safety, and freedom of navigation in and overflight above the South China Sea. The statement also referenced the creation of voluntary and binding norms related to responsible state behaviors regarding ICT. The ARF also "took note" of the AOIP, "including its principles of strengthening ASEAN centrality, openness, transparency, inclusivity, a rules-based framework, good governance, respect for sovereignty, equality, mutual respect, mutual trust, mutual benefit, and respect for international law, such as the UN Charter and the 1982 UNCLOS."[316] On the other hand, ASEAN's emphasis on respect for sovereignty generally complicates efforts to advance a democracy support agenda in the ARF and other regional institutions such as the East Asia Summit.

ASEAN PLUS THREE

The "ASEAN Plus Three (APT) Cooperation Work Plan 2018-2022" lists several goals and objectives explicitly related to democracy, such as: "strengthening cooperation to promote good governance, rule of law and promotion of human rights; support for the implementation of the ASEAN Human Rights Declaration (AHRD) and the Phnom Penh Statement on the Adoption of the AHRD ('Phnom Penh Statement'); and exchange of information on regional efforts to advance human rights and fundamental freedoms in ASEAN." There are also sections with objectives related to women's empowerment and gender equality, building civil service capacity, and promoting cooperation on labor and migrant workers.[317]

ASIAN DEVELOPMENT BANK

Australia, India, Indonesia, Japan, South Korea, Taiwan, and the United States are all founding members of the Asian Development Bank (ADB), and Japan is the top contributor to the ADB annually. Moreover, the United States and Japan have majority ownership of the bank.[318] U.S. and Japanese leadership in the ADB is often seen as a counter to the Chinese-led Asia Infrastructure and Investment Bank (AIIB). In 2018, operational plans for the ADB Strategy 2030 were launched with the aim of achieving prosperous, inclusive, resilient, and sustainable growth in Asia and the Pacific. Important areas of operational focus include "tackling social and gender inequalities, developing sustainable and quality infrastructure, mitigating and adapting to climate change, improving institutional capacity of governments, and furthering regional integration."[319] These development objectives are aligned with the SDGs.[320] The ADB is instrumental in promoting regional collaboration and has identified many democratic norms as priority areas.

ASIA-PACIFIC ECONOMIC COOPERATION

Asia-Pacific Economic Cooperation (APEC), with its focus on capacity-building projects, is another regional economic forum that can be leveraged to further a democracy support agenda. The Senior Officials' Meeting in March 2021 emphasized advancing digital inclusion, infrastructure, and green technology as a part of regional Covid-19 recovery.[321] The 2020 Renewed APEC Agenda for Structural Reform included a focus on open and competitive markets; more inclusive markets, including the participation of small businesses, women, youth, and people with disabilities; and sustainable social policies.[322] APEC has an Anti-Corruption and Transparency working group aiming to counter corruption and promote good governance, market integrity, and enhanced trade in the Indo-Pacific region.[323] The Policy Partnership on Women in the Economy advances the economic integration of women in the APEC region, recognizing the potential for women's economic contribution.[324] Japan and Australia played leading roles in establishing APEC and have since promoted the free economic regionalism embodied in the forum. Australia and the United States have advocated for India to be included in APEC.

INDIAN OCEAN RIM ASSOCIATION

The Indian Ocean Rim Association (IORA) is another multilateral organization aimed at regional cooperation and sustainable development, with a focus on the Indian Ocean region. India and Australia are founding members of the IORA. Membership was extended to Indonesia in 1996, and the United States, Japan, and South Korea are dialogue partners. The first IORA strategic planning workshop, held in 2019, focused on implementing the "IORA Action Plan 2017–2021," strengthening regional collaboration, building international partnerships, and deepening engagement with dialogue partners, among others.[325] Women's economic empowerment is also included as a special focus area.

Global Institutions

UNITED NATIONS

There is a preference in India, Japan, and Australia for utilizing the United Nations as a funding stream for democracy-related ODA.[326] This is especially true for India and Japan when related to NGO-led projects, as they adhere to principles of noninterference in domestic politics. Similarly, trends in South Korea, Indonesia, and Taiwan are pointing toward increased levels of funding for multilateral institutions in general.

Funding Trends

In 2020, the United States and India were the top two contributors to the UN Democracy Fund (UNDEF), funding nearly half (48.78 percent) of the cumulative $214.9 million budget from 2005 to 2020. However, India's UNDEF contributions have decreased drastically since 2013, from an average of $5 million in annual contributions to roughly $100,000. Japan, Australia, and South Korea rank fifth, seventh, and eleventh, respectively in UNDEF contributions from 2005 to 2020, totaling a combined $20,772,424 (9.67 percent) of the cumulative budget. In addition, India, Australia, and Japan share a focus on women's empowerment and ending violence against women.[327]

Australia

In 2020-21, Australia provided AUD 12.725 million (approximately $9.586 million) in core funding to the UNDP, AUD 21 million (approximately $16 million) in core funding to the United Nations Children's Fund (UNICEF), and AUD 1.5 million (approximately $1.1 million) to the United Nations Volunteers Programme.[328]

Australia provides both core and non-core funding to the UNDP. In 2019, Australian funding to the UNDP supported people in crisis-affected countries to get a job or a better livelihood; helped people register to vote; and provided aid for women to gain access to basic services, financial services, and non-financial assets. In 2020, Australian funding contributed to health security, stability, and economic recovery related to Covid-19.[329]

From 2020 to 2022, Australia is providing AUD 10 million (approximately $7.5 million) to UN Women to support activities focused on prevention, essential services, and support for local women's organizations to end violence against women and girls.[330] Australia also funds the UN Office on Drugs and Crime (UNODC) to strengthen anti-corruption legislative, regulatory, and policy frameworks in South and Southeast Asia.[331]

India

India supports women's empowerment through UN Women in India, a UN project staffed by officials in New Delhi that works to end violence against women, promote female leadership and participation, engage in planning and budgeting, promote economic empowerment, and achieve peace and security across the region.[332] As mentioned above, India is also a major contributor to UNDEF, and from 2006 to 2015, India's financial contributions to UNDEF totaled $31.5 million. In that time, India funded 66 NGO-led projects across Afghanistan, Bangladesh, Bhutan, Myanmar, the Maldives, Nepal, Pakistan, and Sri Lanka.[333]

India also hosts the India International Institute on Democracy and Electoral Management (IIDEM) with the United Nations, the Commonwealth, and intergovernmental institutions. Through the IIDEM, India has sent election officials to assist in conducting polls and observing elections and has supplied electronic voting machines, vehicles, and other material to Afghanistan, Bhutan, the Maldives, Egypt, and Tunisia.[334]

Indonesia

Indonesia's establishment in 2019 of the Indonesian Agency for International Development (Indo AID) is seen as a way of making a more significant contribution to international development cooperation and foreign aid disbursement. Indo AID plans to focus on assistance in times of natural disasters and humanitarian crises, on reducing poverty and social inequality, and on increasing Indonesia's participation in the SDGs. Accordingly, Indonesia's UN efforts related to democracy may be enhanced.[335]

Japan

Japan is another large contributor to the United Nations, especially to the UNDP, UN Women, and UNDEF. Japan contributed $10 million in 2007 to the UNDEF to fund NGOs promoting democracy and human rights.[336] In 2020, Japan was the thirteenth-largest regular resources contributor to UN Women, with $3.9 million, and the sixth-largest total government contributor, with $22.6 million.[337] Japan works with the UNDP and the UN Refugee Agency (UNHCR) on democracy-related projects. Japan also made contributions to help create the UN Human Security Trust Fund, which funds NGOs focused on humanitarian causes. Lastly, UN Asia and the Far East Institute for the

Prevention of Crime and the Treatment of Offenders have a close working relationship with Japan's Ministry of Justice.[338]

South Korea

Unlike its DAC counterparts, only 25 percent of South Korea's ODA is channeled as core funding to multilateral institutions, compared to the DAC average of 41 percent. This share has not changed much since South Korea joined the DAC in 2010. The government has said it intends to expand multilateral collaboration in response to global challenges, which include climate change and humanitarian crises. In 2016, South Korea published a "Multilateral Aid Strategy" identifying five UN agencies to collaborate with based on its policy focus: the UNDP, World Food Programme, UNICEF, World Health Organization, and UNHCR.[339]

Given KOICA's shift toward more explicit democracy-related ODA, South Korea could engage more with the United Nations and other multilateral institutions.[340]

Taiwan

While not a member of the United Nations, Taiwan has worked to help other countries meet the SDGs through its ODA programs. The percentage of Taiwanese ODA given to multilateral institutions such as APEC and the ADB has been increasing over the past decade and accounted for 15 percent of Taiwan's ODA budget in 2017.[341] Taiwan's multilateral aid also goes to relatively minor organizations, such as the Republic of China-Central American Economic Development Fund, the Asia Productivity Organization, the Food and Fertilizer Technology Center, and the Asia Pacific Association of Agriculture Research Institutions.[342] As Taiwan continues to seek UN inclusion and diplomatic recognition through increased integration in international organizations, coordination on UN efforts related to democracy may be possible.

INTERGOVERNMENTAL ORGANIZATIONS

G7

In 2019, the G7 addressed topics related to democracy, including gender equality.[343] French president Emmanuel Macron was able to secure unanimous G7 backing for Reporters without Borders' "Partnership on Information and Democracy," which proclaims basic principles for the global online information and communication space, with the aim of encouraging freely reported and trustworthy news and information.[344] The G7 has also been used as a forum for making statements denouncing human rights abuses and actions that erode democracy, such as the G7 statement on Hong Kong.[345]

This trend toward greater inclusion of a democracy support agenda has continued with the most recent G7 summit hosted in Cornwall in June 2021. The G7 summit communiqué shared the group's agenda for global action, which includes embracing democratic values such as freedom, the rule of law, respect for human rights, and gender equality.[346] Under the area of global responsibility and international action, the G7 countries committed to "increase cooperation on supporting democracy, including through strengthening the G7 Rapid Response Mechanism to counter foreign threats to democracy including disinformation" as well as to "strengthen media freedom and ensure the protection of journalists."[347] The statement also condemns the military coup in Myanmar and calls for a humanitarian response to the situation.[348] Moreover, Australia, India, South Africa, and South Korea were all invited to attend the G7 Summit, and they signed the 2021 Open Societies Statement together with the G7. This statement reaffirmed the countries' commitment to democratic values and norms such as human rights, free and fair elections, freedom of expression, the rule of law, independent judicial systems, and diverse civil society.[349]

D-10

The United Kingdom has been promoting the creation of a D-10—a group of the world's 10 leading democracies—to include all of the G7 members plus South Korea, India, and Australia. The idea complements the Biden administration's effort to coordinate democracy support efforts under the Summit for Democracy, but it is not yet clear how this proposed grouping might evolve.[350] There has been no official news on the D-10, and no official meeting took place during the G7 Summit in June 2021.

ENDNOTES

Executive Summary

1   Michael J. Green et al., *The Sunnylands Principles on Enhancing Democratic Partnership in the Indo-Pacific Region* (Washington, DC: CSIS, July 2020), https://csis-website-prod.s3.amazonaws.com/s3fs-public/publication/20710_Green_FullReport_v2_WEB%20FINAL.pdf.

Foreword

2   Green et al., *The Sunnylands Principles*.

3   Task Force on US Strategy to Support Democracy and Counter Authoritarianism, *Reversing the Tide: Towards a New US Strategy to Support Democracy and Counter Authoritarianism* (Washington, DC: Freedom House, CSIS, and the McCain Institute, April 2021), https://www.csis.org/analysis/reversing-tide.

4   "Mapping the Future of U.S. China Policy: Views of U.S. Thought Leaders, the U.S. Public, and U.S. Allies and Partners," CSIS, October 2020, https://chinasurvey.csis.org/; Michael J. Green et al., *Powers, Norms, and Institutions: The Future of the Indo-Pacific from a Southeast Asia Perspective* (Washington, DC: CSIS, June 2020), https://www.csis.org/analysis/powers-norms-and-institutions-future-indo-pacific-southeast-asia-perspective; and Michael J. Green and Nicholas Szechenyi, *Power and Order in Asia: A Survey of Regional Expectations* (Washington, DC: CSIS, July 2014), https://www.csis.org/analysis/power-and-order-asia.

Australia: "Friendly Neighbor"

5   Joint Standing Committee on Foreign Affairs, Defence and Trade, *First Report - Inquiry into Australia's aid program in the Indo-Pacific* (Canberra: Parliament of the Commonwealth of Australia, April 2019), https://parlinfo.aph.gov.au/parlInfo/download/committees/reportjnt/024253/toc_pdf/Firstreport.pdf;fileType=application%2Fpdf.

6   Department of Foreign Affairs and Trade, *2017 Foreign Policy White Paper* (Canberra: Government of Australia, 2017), https://www.dfat.gov.au/publications/minisite/2017-foreign-policy-white-paper/fpwhitepaper/foreign-policy-white-paper.html.

7   Conversions from AUD to USD in this report were made on November 1, 2021, at an AUD/USD exchange rate of 0.7525. Department of Foreign Affairs and Trade, *Partnerships for Recovery - Australian Official Development Assistance* (Canberra: Government of Australia, 2020), https://www.dfat.gov.au/sites/default/files/pbs-2020-21-dfat-aid-budget-summary.pdf.

8   "Australia," Development Co-operation Profiles, OECD, June 14, 2021, https://www.oecd-ilibrary.org/development/development-co-operation-profiles_7c99890b-en.

9   "Australian Foreign Aid," Lowy Institute, 2016, https://www.lowyinstitute.org/issues/australian-foreign-aid.

10 Department of Foreign Affairs and Trade, *Partnerships for Recovery*.

11 Department of Foreign Affairs and Trade, *2017 Foreign Policy White Paper*, 24.

12 Ibid., 89.

13 Ibid., 25.

14 Joint Standing Committee on Foreign Affairs, Defence and Trade, *First Report*.

15 Jonathan Pryke, "DFAT Cuts Show Our Foreign Policy's Khaki Tinge," Lowy Institute, July 20, 2020, https://www.lowyinstitute.org/publications/dfat-cuts-show-our-foreign-policy-khaki-tinge.

16 Ibid.

17 Ibid.

18 "Creditor Reporting System," OECD, https://stats.oecd.org/Index.aspx?DataSetCode=crs1#. Data was calculated by comparing ODA for "I.5.a. Government & Civil Society-general, Total" between 2010 and 2019.

19 Joint Standing Committee on Foreign Affairs, Defence and Trade, *First Report*.

20 "Australia," Development Co-operation Profiles, OECD.

21 "Development assistance: governance," Government of Australia, Department of Foreign Affairs and Trade, https://www.dfat.gov.au/aid/topics/investment-priorities/governance.

22 Ibid.

23 Ibid.

24 Ibid.

25 Department of Foreign Affairs and Trade (DFAT), *Indo-Pacific Justice and Security Program: Mid-Term Review* (Canberra: Government of Australia, March 2021), https://www.dfat.gov.au/publications/development/indo-pacific-justice-and-security-program-mid-term-evaluation.

26 Ibid.

27 "Partnerships for Recovery and gender equality," Government of Australia, DFAT, n.d., https://www.dfat.gov.au/aid/topics/investment-priorities/gender-equality-empowering-women-girls/partnerships-for-recovery-and-gender-equality.

28 Ibid.

29 "Pacific Regional - Empowering women and girls," Government of Australia, DFAT, n.d., https://www.dfat.gov.au/aid/topics/investment-priorities/gender-equality-empowering-women-girls/pacific-regional-gender-equality-empowering-women-girls.

30 DFAT, *Mid-Term EVALUATION of the Pacific Women Parliamentary Partnerships Project 2013-2018* (Canberra: Government of Australia, March 2017), https://www.dfat.gov.au/sites/default/files/pacific-women-parliamentary-partnerships-project-2013-18-mid-term-evaluation.pdf.

31 "Understanding Women's Political and Administrative Leadership in the Pacific," Pacific Women Shaping Pacific Development, November 25, 2016, https://pacificwomen.org/stories-of-change/understanding-womens-political-and-administrative-leadership-in-the-pacific/.

32 "Pacific Regional - Empowering women and girls," Government of Australia.

33 "FAQs – Design of a new regional gender equality program for the Pacific," Pacific Women Shaping Pacific Development, April 15, 2021, https://pacificwomen.org/news/pacific-women-lead-design-faqs/.

34 "Stabilisation and recovery," Government of Australia, DFAT, n.d., https://www.dfat.gov.au/aid/topics/investment-priorities/building-resilience/stabilisation-and-recovery/Pages/stabilisation-and-recovery.

35   "Stability in Papua New Guinea," Government of Australia, DFAT, n.d., https://www.dfat.gov.au/geo/papua-new-guinea/development-assistance/Pages/governance-assistance-png.

36   DFAT, *Australian NGO Cooperation Program (ANCP) Manual - Section 7.9 Partner Capacity Building Programming* (Canberra: Government of Australia, March 2020), https://www.dfat.gov.au/sites/default/files/ancp-manual-march-2020-v2.pdf.

37   Arnaldo Pellini et al., *Supporting strong, effective and inclusive sub-national governments in Nepal* (Canberra: Asia Foundation and the Government of Australia, DFAT, January 2020), https://www.dfat.gov.au/sites/default/files/2020-01/mid-term-review-dfat-taf-strategic-partnership-on-sub-national-governance-program.pdf.

38   Australian Election Commission, *Australian Electoral Commission Annual Report 2019-20* (Canberra: Government of Australia, 2020), https://www.transparency.gov.au/annual-reports/australian-electoral-commission/reporting-year/2019-20-13.

39   Ibid.

40   "Australia will promote and protect freedom of expression," Government of Australia, DFAT, n.d., https://www.dfat.gov.au/international-relations/international-organisations/un/unhrc-2018-2020/pillars-and-priorities/Pages/australia-will-promote-and-protect-freedom-of-expression.

41   "Civil society engagement and opportunities," Government of Australia, DFAT, n.d., https://www.dfat.gov.au/international-relations/international-organisations/un/unhrc-2018-2020/civil-society-engagement.

42   "Our commitment to human rights," Government of Australia, DFAT, n.d., https://www.dfat.gov.au/international-relations/themes/human-rights/Pages/human-rights.

43   Ibid.

44   "Civil society engagement and opportunities," Government of Australia.

45   "Australia Assists," Government of Australia, DFAT, n.d., https://www.dfat.gov.au/aid/topics/investment-priorities/building-resilience/australia-assists/australia-assists.

46   "Private sector development," Government of Australia, DFAT, n.d., https://www.dfat.gov.au/aid/topics/development-issues/private-sector-development.

47   "Direct Aid Program," Government of Australia, DFAT, n.d., https://www.dfat.gov.au/people-to-people/direct-aid-program/direct-aid-program.

48   "The Australian NGO Cooperation Program (ANCP) 2019-20 Fact Sheet," Government of Australia, DFAT, 2019, https://www.dfat.gov.au/about-us/publications/aid/Pages/the-australian-ngo-cooperation-program-fact-sheet.

49   "Australian Aid: Friendship Grants Guideline - Round 2," Government of Australia, DFAT, July 2019, https://www.dfat.gov.au/sites/default/files/aafg-round-2-guidelines.pdf.

50   "Business Partnerships Platform," Government of Australia, DFAT, n.d., https://www.dfat.gov.au/aid/who-we-work-with/private-sector-partnerships/bpp/business-partnerships-platform.

51   "About," Australian Council for International Development, n.d., https://acfid.asn.au/about.

52   "About Us," International Centre for Democratic Partnerships, n.d., https://www.icdp.com.au/about-us/.

53   "Who We Are," CARE Australia, n.d., https://www.care.org.au/who-we-are/.

54 "Our Work," International Women's Development Agency, n.d., https://iwda.org.au/what-we-do/.

55 "Solidarity Across Borders: The Story of Union Aid Abroad – APHEDA," Union Aid Abroad—APHEDA, n.d., https://www.apheda.org.au/history/.

Japan: "Good Governance Leader"

56 Atsuko Geiger, *Japan's Support for Democracy-Related Issues: Mapping Survey* (Tokyo: Japan Center for International Exchange, 2019), https://www.jcie.org/wp-content/uploads/2019/10/Japan-Democracy-Survey-2019_FINAL.pdf.

57 Hironori Sasada, "Resurgence of the 'Japan Model': Japan's Aid Policy Reform and Infrastructure Development Assistance," *Asian Survey* 59, no. 6 (November/December 2019): 1044–1069, doi:10.1525/as.2019.59.6.1044.

58 "Japan's Initiatives at the Lyon Summit," Ministry of Foreign Affairs of Japan, June 29, 1996, https://www.mofa.go.jp/policy/economy/summit/1996/initiative.html.

59 Geiger, *Japan's Support For Democracy Related Issues*.

60 Nicholas Szechenyi, ed., *Asianism and Universalism: The Evolution of Norms and Power in Modern Asia* (Washington, DC: CSIS, 2019), 7–8, https://www.csis.org/analysis/asianism-and-universalism-evolution-norms-and-power-modern-asia.

61 Government of Japan, *National Security Strategy* (Tokyo: December 2013), http://japan.kantei.go.jp/96_abe/documents/2013/__icsFiles/afieldfile/2013/12/17/NSS.pdf.

62 The charter states: "Japan will pay adequate attention to the situation in the recipient countries regarding the process of democratization, the rule of law and the protection of basic human rights, with a view to promoting the consolidation of democratization, the rule of law and the respect for basic human rights." See Government of Japan, *Cabinet decision on the Development Cooperation Charter* (Tokyo: February 2015), https://www.mofa.go.jp/files/000067701.pdf.

63 The first reason is that Japan wants to maintain the status quo—and the liberal international order—amid China's rise, through support of international rule of law. Commitment to the rule of law also contributes to the maintenance of the maritime status quo in Asia, which Japan is invested in given its territorial dispute with China. Second, democracy support is linked to growing Chinese security concerns, as evidenced by the "Arc of Freedom and Prosperity" in the 2013 National Security Strategy. The use of the term "democracy" is seen as a tool for uniting other democratic countries together to form a security community and encouraging defense cooperation with democratic security partners. Lastly, Japan is emphasizing its presence as a liberal democracy and differentiating itself from China as part of its overall effort to strengthen its influence in the region. See more in Szechenyi, *Asianism and Universalism*; and Geiger, *Japan's Support for Democracy-Related Issues*.

64 Geiger, *Japan's Support for Democracy-Related Issues*.

65 Maiko Ichihara, "International Power Structure and Strategic Motivations: Democracy Support from Japan and Indonesia" JICA Research Institute, Working Paper 194, August 2019, https://www.jica.go.jp/jica-ri/publication/workingpaper/wp_194.html.

66 Geiger, *Japan's Support for Democracy-Related Issues*.

67 Maiko Ichihara, *The Changing Role of Democracy in Asian Geopolitics* (Washington, DC: Carnegie Endowment for International Peace, September 2017), https://carnegieendowment.org/2017/09/14/changing-role-of-democracy-in-asian-geopolitics-pub-73110.

68 "Creditor Reporting System," OECD.

69 Conversions from JPY to USD in this report were made on November 1, 2021, at a USD/JYP exchange rate of 114.00. Geiger, *Japan's Support for Democracy-Related Issues*.

70 Ibid.

71 Ibid.

72 Geiger, *Japan's Support for Democracy-Related Issues*; and "ERIA and AIPA Sign MOU to Support ASEAN Parliamentary Members," Economic Research Institute for ASEAN and East Asia, December 21, 2016, http://www.eria.org/news-and-views/eria-and-aipa-sign-mou-to-support-asean-parliamentary-members/.

73 "Project for Capacity Development on Training Management for Strengthening Sub-National Administrations," Japan International Cooperation Agency, June 30, 2020, https://www.jica.go.jp/cambodia/english/office/topics/200630_01.html.

74 "Gender and Development" in Japan International Cooperation Agency (JICA), *JICA Annual Report 2020* (Tokyo: November 2020), https://www.jica.go.jp/english/publications/reports/annual/2020/index.html.

75 Ibid.

76 "Gender and Development: Training Programs," JICA, n.d., https://www.jica.go.jp/english/our_work/thematic_issues/gender/background/training.html.

77 Ibid.

78 Geiger, *Japan's Support for Democracy-Related Issues*.

79 Ibid.

80 "Creditor Reporting System," OECD.

81 Yasunobu Sato, "Japan's Approach to Global Democracy Support: Focused on Law and Judicial Reform Assistance," in *U.S.-Japan Approaches to Democracy Promotion*, edited by Michael R. Auslin and Daniel E. Bob (Washington, DC: Sasakawa Peace Foundation USA, 2017), https://spfusa.org/wp-content/uploads/2017/03/Sasakawa_Democracy.pdf.

82 JICA, *Japan's Approach to Legal and Judicial Development in Developing Countries: Building Trust and Partnership* (Tokyo: Japan Publishing Industry Foundation for Culture, 2020), 17.

83 Ibid., 132.

84 Ibid.

85 Ibid., 17.

86 Geiger, *Japan's Support for Democracy-Related Issues*.

87 Sato, "Japan's Approach to Global Democracy Support."

88 Ibid.

89 "Activities in Viet Nam," JICA, n.d., https://www.jica.go.jp/vietnam/english/activities/index.html.

90 "Legal System Development Support Projects," International Civil and Commercial Law Centre Foundation, n.d., https://www.icclc.or.jp/english/project/; and "JICA'S On-Going Projects Map in Vietnam," JICA, May 2021, https://www.jica.go.jp/vietnam/english/activities/c8h0vm0000anjq56-att/ongoing_en.pdf.

91 Geiger, *Japan's Support for Democracy-Related Issues*.

92 "Governance Case Study," JICA, n.d., https://www.jica.go.jp/english/our_work/thematic_issues/governance/study.html.

93   JICA, *Japan's Approach to Legal and Judicial Development in Developing Countries*, 148.

94   Ibid.

95   Ibid.

96   Ibid., 227.

97   Ibid.

98   Ibid., 239.

99   Ibid., 236.

100 Ibid.

101 Ibid.

102 Geiger, *Japan's Support for Democracy-Related Issues*.

103 Sato, "Japan's Approach to Global Democracy Support."

104 Ichihara, "International Power Structure and Strategic Motivations."

105 Geiger, *Japan's Support for Democracy-Related Issues*.

106 Sato, "Japan's Approach to Global Democracy Support."

107 Ibid.

108 "Overview," JICA Development Studies Program, n.d., https://www.jica.go.jp/dsp-chair/english/dsp/overview/index.html.

109 "Southeast Asia and the Pacific" in JICA, *JICA Annual Report 2020* (Tokyo: November 2020), https://www.jica.go.jp/english/publications/reports/annual/2020/c8h0vm0000fc7q2b-att/2020_05.pdf.

110 "Save the Date! C20 Summit will be held in 21-23 April 2019 in Tokyo, Japan," JANIC, January 30, 2019, https://www.janic.org/en/2019/01/30/c20_summit_date/.

111 C20 2019 Secretariat, *C20 2019 Final Report* (Tokyo: C20 2019 Secretariat, November 2019), https://civil-20.org/2019/wp-content/uploads/2019/11/C20-2019-Final-Report.pdf.

112 JANIC, "Call for participation in Tokyo Democracy Forum on 15&16 Feb 2021," press release, February 5, 2021, https://www.janic.org/en/2021/02/05/tokyo_democracy_forum_hapic2021/.

113 Based on confidential interviews with current and formal officials.

114 JICA, *Japan's Approach to Legal and Judicial Development in Developing Countries*, 105.

115 Ibid., 275.

116 Ibid.

117 "Center for Asian Legal Exchange," Nagoya University, n.d., https://en.nagoya-u.ac.jp/about_nu/admin/sch/deta/cale.html.

118 JICA, *Japan's Approach to Legal and Judicial Development in Developing Countries*, 218.

119 Ibid.

120 Ibid.

121 "Democracy Dialogue," Genron NPO, n.d., https://www.genron-npo.net/en/pp/category/286.html.

122 Yasushi Kudo, "Putting democracy back in the hands of the people," Genron NPO, April 13, 2021, https://www.genron-npo.net/en/pp/archives/5578.html.

123 Nippon Foundation Group, *Projects in Myanmar* (Tokyo: Nippon Foundation, June 1, 2020), https://www.nippon-foundation.or.jp/app/uploads/2019/01/en_wha_pro_mya_01.pdf.

India: "Election Expert"

124 Niha Masih, "Election Workers in India Traveled 300 Miles over 4 Days to Set up a Polling Booth - for One Voter," *Washington Post*, April 17, 2019, https://www.washingtonpost.com/world/asia_pacific/election-workers-in-india-traveled-300-miles-over-4-days-to-set-up-a-polling-booth--for-one-voter/2019/04/17/44b4eb46-5bb1-11e9-98d4-844088d135f2_story.html.

125 Tariq Ahmad, *National Parliaments: India* (Washington, DC: Library of Congress, February 2017), https://tile.loc.gov/storage-services/service/ll/llglrd/2016478967/2016478967.pdf.

126 Yeshi Choedon, "India and Democracy Promotion," *India Quarterly: A Journal of International Affairs* 71, no. 2 (2015): 160–173, doi:10.1177/0974928414568618; Pratap Bhanu Mehta, "Do New Democracies Support Democracy? Reluctant India," *Journal of Democracy* 22, no. 4 (2011): 97–109, https://www.journalofdemocracy.org/articles/do-new-democracies-support-democracy-reluctant-india/.

127 Mehta, "Do New Democracies Support Democracy? Reluctant India."

128 Choedon, "India and Democracy Promotion."

129 Shivshankar Menon, *India's Foreign Affairs Strategy* (New Delhi: Brookings India, May 2020), https://www.brookings.edu/wp-content/uploads/2020/05/India27s-foreign-affairs-strategy.pdf.

130 S.D. Muni, *Supporting Democracy Abroad – India* (Washington, DC: Freedom House, December 2014), https://www.refworld.org/docid/5497f82715.html.

131 Ian Hall, "Not Promoting, Not Exporting: India's Democracy Assistance," *Rising Powers Quarterly* 2, no. 3 (2017): 81–97, https://www.orfonline.org/research/not-promoting-exporting-india-democracy-assistance/.

132 Ibid.

133 Uzair Younus, "The Power of Example: Democracy Assistance in Indian Foreign Policy," Stimson Center, November 23, 2020, https://www.stimson.org/2020/the-power-of-example-democracy-assistance-in-indian-foreign-policy/.

134 Subhash Agrawal, "Emerging Donors in International Development Assistance: The India Case," Partnership in 92 Business and Development Division, December 2007, https://idl-bnc-idrc.dspacedirect.org/bitstream/handle/10625/57511/IDL-57511.pdf?sequence=2&isAllowed=y.

135 Hall, "Not Promoting, Not Exporting."

136 Choedon, "India and Democracy Promotion."

137 Hall, "Not Promoting, Not Exporting."

138 Ibid.

139 Mehta, "Do New Democracies Support Democracy? Reluctant India."

140 Listed in "Grants and Loans to Foreign Governments" under "Expenditure Profile 2021-2022," Ministry of Finance, Union Budget (New Delhi: Government of India, 2020), https://www.indiabudget.gov.in/doc/eb/stat20.pdf.

141 Ministry of External Affairs, *Annual Report 2020-21* (New Delhi: Government of India, 2020–21), 224, http://www.mea.gov.in/Uploads/PublicationDocs/33569_MEA_annual_Report.pdf.

142 Conversions from Indian rupees to USD in this report were made on November 1, 2021, at a USD/INR exchange rate of 74.8363. Listed in "Ministry of External Affairs" under "Notes on Demands for Grants, 2020-2021," Ministry of Finance, *Union Budget* (New Delhi: Government of India, 2020), https://www.indiabudget.gov.in/budget2020-21/doc/eb/sbe26.pdf.

143 "Partnership for Gender Equality: India," U.S. Agency for International Development, July 17, 2019, https://www.usaid.gov/india/gender-equality.

144 Ibid.

145 Ibid.

146 "International Cooperation," Election Commission of India, n.d., https://eci.gov.in/divisions-of-eci/international-cooperation/.

147 Daniel Calingaert, Arch Puddington, and Sarah Repucci, *The Democracy Support Deficit: Despite Progress, Major Countries Fall Short* (Washington, DC: Freedom House, 2014), https://freedomhouse.org/sites/default/files/2020-02/GSD_Overview_and_Country_Reports.pdf.

148 "International Cooperation," Election Commission of India.

149 Ibid.

150 Hall, "Not Promoting, Not Exporting."

151 Ibid.

152 Anil Bhuimali, *India's Approach to Foreign Aid* (Glasgow: University of Glasgow/Raiganj University, 2018), https://www.gla.ac.uk/media/Media_619372_smxx.pdf.

153 "India-Africa Cooperation in Science and Technology – Capacity Building," Ministry of External Affairs, Government of India, October 2015, https://www.mea.gov.in/infocus-article.htm?25947/IndiaAfrica+cooperation+in+science+and+Technology+; and Bhuimali, *India's Approach to Foreign Aid*.

154 Bhuimali, *India's Approach to Foreign Aid*.

155 Ministry of External Affairs, *Annual Report: 2019-2020* (New Delhi: Government of India, 2020), http://www.mea.gov.in/Uploads/PublicationDocs/32489_AR_Spread_2020_new.Pdf.

156 Muni, "Supporting Democracy Abroad – India."

157 Ibid.

158 Lok Sabha Secretariat, *Bureau of Parliamentary Studies and Training* (New Delhi: overnment of India, May 2014), http://164.100.47.194/our%20parliament/Bureau%20of%20parliamentary%20studies.pdf; and "Aims, Objects and Activities," Parliamentary Research and Training Institute for Democracies, n.d., http://164.100.47.194/bpstnew/aim1.aspx.

159 "Calendar of Events," Parliamentary Research and Training Institute for Democracies, last updated September 14, 2021, http://164.100.47.194/bpstnew/Program_master.aspx.

160 Ibid.

161 Saneet Chakradeo, *Neighbourhood First Responder: India's Humanitarian Assistance and Disaster Relief* (Washington, DC: Brookings, August 2020), https://www.brookings.edu/

research/neighbourhood-first-responder-indias-humanitarian-assistance-and-disaster-relief/.

162 Ibid.

163 Constantino Xavier and Riya Sinha, *When Land Comes in the Way: India's Connectivity Infrastructure in Nepal* (Washington, DC: Brookings, August 2020), https://www.brookings.edu/wp-content/uploads/2020/08/When-land-comes-in-the-way_M-1.pdf.

164 Agrawal, "Emerging Donors in International Development Assistance."

165 Ibid.

166 Ibid.

167 "Lines of Credit," India Exim Bank, August 13, 2021, https://www.eximbankindia.in/lines-of-credit.

Indonesia: "ASEAN Organizer"

168 Hassan Wirajuda, "Democracy and Diplomacy," *New Zealand International Review* 37, no. 2 (2012): 7–10, doi:10.2307/45235474.

169 Amitav Acharya, *Indonesia Matters: Asia's Emerging Democratic Power* (Singapore: World Scientific, 2015), 1–2.

170 Wirajuda, "Democracy and Diplomacy."

171 ASEAN, *The ASEAN Charter* (Jakarta: November 2007), 3–6, https://asean.org/wp-content/uploads/2012/05/11.-October-2015-The-ASEAN-Charter-18th-Reprint-Amended-updated-on-05_-April-2016-IJP.pdf.

172 Gibran Mahesa Drajat, "Assessing Indonesia's Leadership in the Advancement of ASEAN Political Security Community under President Joko Widodo," *AEGIS: Journal of International Relations* 2, no. 2 (2018): 147, http://e-journal.president.ac.id/presunivojs/index.php/AEGIS/article/view/424/.

173 ASEAN, *ASEAN Human Rights Declaration* (Jakarta: November 2012), https://asean.org/asean-human-rights-declaration/.

174 Ichihara, "The Changing Role of Democracy in Asian Geopolitics."

175 "Indonesia, Malaysia ask ASEAN to hold special meeting on Myanmar," Xinhua, February 5, 2021, http://www.xinhuanet.com/english/asiapacific/2021-02/05/c_139724254.htm.

176 Donald Weatherbee, *Indonesia in ASEAN: Vision and Reality* (Singapore: Institute of Southeast Asian Studies, 2013), 30.

177 Jet Damazo-Santos, "What has the Bali Democracy Forum achieved?," Rappler, October 11, 2014, https://www.rappler.com/world/asia-pacific/bali-democracy-forum.

178 Mohamad Rosyidin, "Promoting a home-grown democracy: Indonesia's approach of democracy promotion in the Bali democracy Forum (BDF)," *Asian Journal of Political Science* 28, no.3 (September 2020): 312–333, doi:10.1080/02185377.2020.1814361.

179 Ibid.

180 Ibid.

181 Lina A. Alexandra and Marc Lanteigne, "New Actors and Innovative Approaches to Peacebuilding: The Case of Myanmar," in *Rising Powers and Peacebuilding*, edited by Charles T. Call and Cedric de Coning (New York: Palgrave Macmillan, Cham., 2017), doi:10.1007/978-3-319-60621-7_9.

182 Ministry of Foreign Affairs of the Republic of Indonesia, "Bali Civil Society and Media orum 2020, Where International Civil Society Organizations and Media Exchange Ideas on Democracy and the Pandemic," press release, October 21, 2020, https://kemlu.go.id/portal/en/read/1814/berita/bali-civil-society-and-media-forum-2020-where-international-civil-society-organizations-and-media-exchange-ideas-on-democracy-and-the-pandemic.

183 Alexandra and Lanteigne, "New Actors and Innovative Approaches to Peacebuilding."

184 Ibid.

185 Ibid.

186 Susan Lee and Mi Ki Kyaw Myint, "Myanmar Election Commission Visits Indonesia," Asia Foundation, May 20, 2015, https://asiafoundation.org/2015/05/20/myanmar-election-commission-visits-indonesia/.

187 "Indonesia invites foreign observers to monitor 2019 elections," Xinhua, March 25, 20219, http://www.xinhuanet.com/english/2019-03/25/c_137922490.htm.

188 Dian Septiari, "Jokowi, Muhyiddin call for special ASEAN meeting on Myanmar," *Jakarta Post*, February 5, 2021, https://www.thejakartapost.com/seasia/2021/02/05/jokowi-muhyiddin-call-for-special-asean-meeting-on-myanmar.html.

189 Alexandra and Lanteigne, "New Actors and Innovative Approaches to Peacebuilding."

190 Ralf Emmers, "Democratization, National Identity and Indonesia's Foreign Policy," The Asan Forum, June 25, 2019, https://theasanforum.org/democratization-national-identity-and-indonesias-foreign-policy/.

191 "About the Habibie Center," Habibie Center, n.d., https://www.habibiecenter.or.id/profil.

192 "Event," Habibie Center, n.d., https://www.habibiecenter.or.id/event.

South Korea: "Important Middle Power"

193 Ichihara, "The Changing Role of Democracy in Asian Geopolitics."

194 Conversions from KRW to USD in this report were made on November 1, 2021, at a USD/KRW exchange rate of 1,177.58. Korea International Cooperation Agency (KOICA), *KOICA Annual Report 2018* (Seoul: 2018), 29, http://www.koica.go.kr/koica_en/3492/subview.do.

195 "The Republic of Korea's Country Partnership Strategy for the People's Republic of Bangladesh 2016-2020," Korea Official Development Assistance, March 2017, https://www.odakorea.go.kr/contentFile/CPS(eng)/BGD.pdf.

196 Jongryn Mo, "South Korea's middle power diplomacy: A case of growing compatibility between regional and global roles," *International Journal* 71, no. 4 (December 2016): 587–607, https://www.jstor.org/stable/26414059.

197 Kim Sung Han, "Northeast Asian Regionalism in Korea" Council on Foreign Relations, December 2009, http://www.nautilus.org/wp-content/uploads/2012/09/NEAsiaSecurityKim.pdf.

198 Simon Bruns, "Democracy Promotion through ODA: The Future of Korean Public Diplomacy?," in *Collection of Essays on Korea's Public Diplomacy: Possibilities and Future Outlook* (Seoul: Ministry of Foreign Affairs, 2020), 401–6.

199 Ibid., 406.

200 Dong-choon Kim et al., "Korea's Experience of Democratic Development at the International Cooperation Perspective: from Recipient to Donor," KOICA, June 2019,

https://www.odakorea.go.kr/fileDownLoad.xdo?f_id=15668684943171921681200YZEZ8
1T61NF2YPUYBCMF.

201 KOICA Strategy and Policy Planning for Development Programs Team, *Mid-to-long term implementation plans of KOICA to achieve SDG 16 [peace, justice, governance]* (Seoul: KOICA, December 2019), http://koica.go.kr/sites/koica_en/download/5_Mid_to_long_Term_Implementation_Plan.pdf.

202 Ibid.

203 Korea Official Development Assistance, *2017 Korea's ODA White Paper: Beautiful Sharing, Wonderful Growing* (Seoul: Committee for International Development Cooperation, December 2017), https://www.odakorea.go.kr/bbs/selectArticleDetail?bbsId=eng_102&nttId=15028&menuNo=12032100; and KOICA, *KOICA Annual Report 2018*.

204 "KOICA Sector: Governance," KOICA, n.d., http://koica.go.kr/koica_en/3416/subview.do.

205 "KOICA Sector: Human Rights & Peace," KOICA, n.d., http://koica.go.kr/koica_en/8007/subview.do.

206 KOICA, *Implementation plan for the ODA strategy of Korea-ASEAN Future Community* (Seoul: KOICA, January 2020), http://www.koica.go.kr/sites/koica_en/download/8_Implementation_Plan.pdf.

207 "The Republic of Korea's Country Partnership Strategy for the Socialist Republic of Vietnam 2016-2020," Korea Official Development Assistance, March 2017, https://www.odakorea.go.kr/bbs/selectArticleDetail?bbsId=eng_102&nttId=15047&menuNo=12032100.

208 KOICA, *KOICA Annual Report 2018*.

209 KOICA, *Detailed document on KOICA's Country Plan* (Seoul: January 2020), http://www.koica.go.kr/sites/koica_en/download/9_Detailed_Document.pdf.

210 KOICA, *Implementation plan for the ODA strategy of Korea-ASEAN Future Community*.

211 "The Republic of Korea's Country Partnership Strategy for the Republic of the Union of Myanmar 2016-2020," Korea Official Development Assistance, March 2017, https://www.odakorea.go.kr/bbs/selectArticleDetail?bbsId=eng_102&nttId=15047&menuNo=12032100.

212 Ibid.

213 KOICA, *KOICA Annual Report 2018*.

214 Ibid.

215 Ibid.

216 KOICA, *Detailed document on KOICA's Country Plan*; KOICA, *Implementation plan for the ODA strategy of Korea-ASEAN Future Community*; and "Project Document – Country: Indonesia," United Nations Development Programme, January 4, 2019, https://info.undp.org/docs/pdc/Documents/IDN/PRODOC%20SP4N%20LAPOR_signed%20by%20CB%20RR%20UNDP%20(Final).pdf.

217 KOICA, *KOICA Annual Report 2018*.

218 KOICA, *Detailed document on KOICA's Country Plan*; and "Country and Sector data (detail)," KOICA STATS, http://stat.koica.go.kr/ipm/os/acms/smrizeAreaList.do?lang=en.

219 Ibid.

220 UN Population Fund Vietnam, "Launch of the KOICA funded project on building a model to respond to Violence Against Women and Girls in Viet Nam," press release,

January 16, 2018, https://vietnam.unfpa.org/en/news/launch-koica-funded-project-building-model-respond-violence-against-women-and-girls-viet-nam.

221 Ministry of Foreign Affairs of the Republic of Korea, "Press Releases: 'Action with Women and Peace' Initiative and Advisory Committee Launched," press release, June 19, 2018, http://www.mofa.go.kr/eng/brd/m_5676/view.do?seq=319914&srchFr=&amp%3BsrchTo=&amp%3BsrchWord=UN&amp%3BsrchTp=0&amp%3Bmulti_itm_seq=0&amp%3Bitm_seq_1=0&amp%3Bitm_seq_2=0&amp%3Bcompany_cd=&amp%3Bcompany_nm=&page=1&titleNm=.

222 Ibid.

223 Ibid.

224 Ministry of Foreign Affairs of the Republic of Korea, "Press Releases: Development Alliance Korea to be Launched," press release, August 9, 2012, http://www.mofa.go.kr/eng/brd/m_5676/view.do?seq=311354&srchFr=&amp%3BsrchTo=&amp%3BsrchWord=&amp%3BsrchTp=0&amp%3Bmulti_itm_seq=0&amp%3Bitm_seq_1=0&amp%3Bitm_seq_2=0&amp%3Bcompany_cd=&amp%3Bcompany_nm=&page=538&titleNm=.

225 Korea Official Development Assistance, *2017 Korea's ODA White Paper*.

226 KOICA, *KOICA Annual Report 2018*.

227 KOICA Strategy and Policy Planning for Development Programs Team, *SDG 16: PEACE Initiative - Initiative for Accelerating SDG 16* (Seoul: KOICA, December 2019), http://koica.go.kr/sites/koica_en/download/6_SDG_16_PEACE_Initiative.pdf.

228 KOICA Strategy and Policy Planning for Development Programs Team, *Mid-to-long term implementation plans*.

229 Ichihara, "The Changing Role of Democracy in Asian Geopolitics."

230 Ibid.

231 "About," Asia Democracy Network, n.d., https://adnasia.org/about/.

232 "ADN Youth Programs," Asia Democracy Network, n.d., https://adnasia.org/programs/2020-asia-youth-assembly/.

233 Ibid.

234 "Asia Democracy Academy," Asia Democracy Academy, n.d., https://asia-democracy-academy.thinkific.com/.

235 "Asia Democracy Forums," Asia Democracy Network, n.d., https://adnasia.org/programs/asia-democracy-forums/.

236 "What is ADRN," Asia Democracy Research Network, n.d., http://www.adrnresearch.org/about/what.php.

237 Ibid.

238 "About," Jeju Forum for Peace and Prosperity, n.d., http://www.jejuforum.or.kr/m11.php; and "Events," Jeju Forum for Peace and Prosperity, 2021, http://www.jejuforum.or.kr/m21_program.php?year=2021.

239 "Joint Statement on U.S.-Japan-ROK Women's Empowerment Trilateral Forum," U.S. Embassy and Consulate in the Republic of Korea, September 27, 2016, https://kr.usembassy.gov/joint-statement-on-u-s-japan-republic-of-korea-womens-empowerment-trilateral-forum/.

Taiwan: "Democracy Diplomat"

240   Taiwan Ministry of Foreign Affairs, *International Cooperation and Development Report 2018* (Taipei: Ministry of Foreign Affairs, 2019), 1-52, https://ws.mofa.gov.tw/Download.ashx?u=LzAwMS9VcGxvYWQvT2xkRmlsZS9SZWxGaWxlLzE3LzI2Mi9hMDkxYzU1MS05ZDBkLTQwMDAtOGMwYy05NzAxMzM2NjBkYzEucGRm&n=5ZyL6Zqb5ZCI5L2c55m85bGV5LqL5YuZMTA35bm05bqm5aCx5ZGKKOiLseaWh%2BJiCkucGRm.

241   "International Grants in 2018," Taiwan Foundation for Democracy, n.d., http://www.tfd.org.tw/opencms/english/grants/international/International0017.html.

242   Joel Atkinson, "Comparing Taiwan's foreign aid to Japan, South Korea and DAC," *Journal of the Asia Pacific Economy* 22, no. 2 (November 2016): 253, doi:10.1080/13547860.2016.1245926.

243   "Background," Taiwan Foundation for Democracy, n.d., http://www.tfd.org.tw/opencms/english/about/background.html.

244   "Introduction of the East Asia Democracy Forum," Taiwan Foundation for Democracy, n.d., http://www.tfd.org.tw/opencms/english/events/data/Event0826.html; and Ichihara, "The Changing Role of Democracy in Asia Geopolitics."

245   "Introduction of the East Asia Democracy Forum," Taiwan Foundation for Democracy.

246   "The Fifth East Asia Democracy Forum in Taipei," Taiwan Foundation for Democracy, June 26, 2018, http://www.tfd.org.tw/opencms/english/events/data/Event0698.html.

247   "The 2019 6th East Asia Democracy Forum," Taiwan foundation for Democracy, June 26, 2019, http://www.tfd.org.tw/opencms/english/events/data/Event0782.html.

248   "East Asia Democracy Forum Statement: Democracy and Civil Society Vital to Addressing Pandemic," Taiwan Foundation for Democracy, July 7, 2021, http://www.tfd.org.tw/opencms/english/events/data/Event0831.html.

249   Taiwan Foundation for Democracy, *2019 Annual Report* (Taipei: Taiwan Foundation for Democracy, 2020), http://www.tfd.org.tw/export/sites/tfd/files/download/2019_AR_EN.pdf.

250   Ibid.

251   Ibid.

252   Denghua Zhang, "Comparing China's and Taiwan's aid to the Pacific," Development Policy Centre, January 20, 2020, https://devpolicy.org/comparing-chinas-and-taiwans-aid-to-the-pacific-20200120/.

253   "2022 Pacific Islands Leadership Program," East-West Center, n.d., https://www.eastwestcenter.org/scholarships-fellowships/2022-pacific-islands-leadership-program; Zhang, "Comparing China's and Taiwan's aid to the Pacific."

254   Taiwan Ministry of Foreign Affairs, *International Cooperation and Development Report 2018*.

255   "Fact Sheet: 2020 U.S.-Taiwan Consultations on Democratic Governance in the Indo-Pacific Region and Beyond," American Institute in Taiwan, October 28, 2020, https://www.ait.org.tw/fact-sheet-2020-us-taiwan-consultations-on-democratic-governance-in-indo-pacific/.

256   Ibid.

257   Ibid.

258   Ibid.

259 Ibid.

260 "Taiwan International and Cooperation Development Fund," Taiwan International and Cooperation Development Fund, n.d., https://www.icdf.org.tw/.

Alpha Case: The United States

261 Marian L. Lawson and Susan B. Epstein, *Democracy Promotion: An Objective of U.S. Foreign Assistance*, CRS Report No. R44858 (Washington, DC: Congressional Research Service, 2019), https://fas.org/sgp/crs/row/R44858.pdf.

262 According to USAID's Agency Financial Reports, the total net cost for the "democracy, human rights, and governance" program area was approximately $1.3 billion in 2017, $1.7 billion in 2018, $1.45 billion in 2019, and $1.6 billion in 2020. See USAID, *Agency Financial Report Fiscal Year 2017: Helping People Progress Beyond Assistance* (Washington, DC: USAID, 2017), https://www.usaid.gov/sites/default/files/documents/1868/USAIDFY2017AFR.pdf; USAID, *Agency Financial Report Fiscal Year 2018: Empowering Communities on Their Development Journey* (Washington, DC: USAID, 2018), https://www.usaid.gov/sites/default/files/documents/1868/USAIDFY2018AFR_508R.pdf; USAID, *Agency Financial Report Fiscal year 2019: Promoting a Path to Self-Reliance and Resilience* (Washington, DC: USAID, 2019), https://www.usaid.gov/sites/default/files/documents/1868/USAIDFY2019AFR_508R.pdf; and USAID, *Agency Financial Report Fiscal Year 2020: A Foundation Built on Decades of Global Health Investment* (Washington, DC: USAID, 2020), https://www.usaid.gov/sites/default/files/documents/USAID_FY2020_AFR-508.pdf.

263 Lawson and Epstein, *Democracy Promotion*.

264 "Fiscal Year (FY) 2022 President's Budget Request for the United States Agency for International Development (USAID)," USAID Budget Fact Sheet, USAID, May 2021, https://www.usaid.gov/sites/default/files/documents/USAID_FY_2022_Budget_Request_Fact_Sheet_May_2021_-_Glossy_-_FINAL.2.pdf.

265 Lawson and Epstein, *Democracy Promotion*.

266 Ibid.

267 "Foreign Assistance Map," Foreign Assistance, n.d., https://www.foreignassistance.gov/.

268 See the National Endowment for Democracy (NED) Award Grant's Search, which includes records of grants NED has awarded in the past three years: "Grant Search," NED, n.d., https://www.ned.org/wp-content/themes/ned/search/grant-search.php?organizationName=&region=&projectCountry=&amount=&fromDate=&toDate=&projectFocus%5B%5D=&search=&maxCount=50&orderBy=Year&start=1&sbmt=1; "IRI Awarded Projects Ending Since Jan 1, 2014," International Research School for Climate and Society, Columbia Climate School, n.d., https://iri.columbia.edu/projects/; and "What we do," NDI, n.d., https://www.ndi.org/what-we-do.

Annex: A Catalogue of Regional Networks and Institutions

269 Mireya Solis, "Japan's democratic renewal and the survival of the liberal order," Brookings Institute, January 22, 2021, https://www.brookings.edu/articles/japans-democratic-renewal-and-the-survival-of-the-liberal-order/.

270 "U.S. Relations With Japan," Bureau of East Asian and Pacific Affairs, U.S. Department of State, January 21, 2020, https://www.state.gov/u-s-relations-with-japan/.

271 Andrew Yeo, "South Korea and the Free and Open Indo-Pacific Strategy," CSIS, July 20, 2020, https://www.csis.org/analysis/south-korea-and-free-and-open-indo-pacific-strategy.

272 "U.S. & ROK Issue a Joint Factsheet on their Regional Cooperation Efforts," U.S. Embassy & Consulate in the Republic of Korea, November 2, 2019, https://kr.usembassy.gov/110219-joint-fact-sheet-by-the-united-states-and-the-republic-of-korea-on-cooperation-between-the-new-southern-policy-and-the-indo-pacific-strategy/.

273 Ibid.

274 "Providing opportunities for Women's Economic Rise," Bureau of Economic and Business Affairs, U.S. Department of State, n.d., https://www.state.gov/womens-economic-empowerment/.

275 "U.S.-ROK Leaders' Joint Statement," The White House, Statements and Releases, May 21, 2021, https://www.whitehouse.gov/briefing-room/statements-releases/2021/05/21/u-s-rok-leaders-joint-statement/.

276 "Memorandum of Understanding for International Development Cooperation between the United States Agency for International Development and the Australian Department of Foreign Affairs and Trade," Australian DFAT, July 28, 2020, https://www.dfat.gov.au/sites/default/files/australia-usa-mou-for-international-development-cooperation.pdf.

277 Ibid.

278 "Joint Statement on Australia-U.S. Ministerial Consultations (AUSMIN) 2021," Office of the Spokesperson, U.S. Department of State, September 16, 2021, https://www.state.gov/joint-statement-on-australia-u-s-ministerial-consultations-ausmin-2021/.

279 Tanvi Madan, "Democracy and the US-India relationship," Brookings Institute, January 22, 2021, https://www.brookings.edu/articles/democracy-and-the-us-india-relationship/; and Richard Youngs, "Upholding Democracy in a Post-Western Order," Carnegie Endowment for International Peace, February 13, 2019, https://carnegieeurope.eu/2019/02/13/upholding-democracy-in-post-western-order-pub-78334.

280 Youngs, "Upholding Democracy in a Post-Western Order."

281 K. V. Kesavan, "India and major powers: Japan," Observer Research Foundation, August 9, 2019, https://www.orfonline.org/expert-speak/india-and-major-powers-japan-54248/; and "Asia Africa Growth Corridor Vision Document," Economic Research Institute for ASEAN and East Asia, May 2017, https://www.eria.org/Asia-Africa-Growth-Corridor-Vision-Document-full.pdf.

282 Australian DFAT, "Joint Statement on a Comprehensive Strategic Partnership between Republic of India and Australia," Australian Government Department of Foreign Affairs and Trade, June 4, 2020, https://www.dfat.gov.au/geo/india/Pages/joint-statement-comprehensive-strategic-partnership-between-republic-india-and-australia.

283 Ibid.

284 Ibid.

285 "International Exchange and Cooperation," Indian Department of Administrative Reforms and Public Grievances, March 3, 2021, https://darpg.gov.in/sites/default/files/Website%20Material%20-%203.3.2021%20%281%29.pdf.

286 Ibid.

287 "Australia-Japan Strategy for Cooperation in the Pacific," Ministry of Foreign Affairs of Japan, February 14, 2016, https://www.mofa.go.jp/files/000134629.pdf.

288 Ibid.

289 Ministry of Foreign Affairs of Japan, "Japan Australia Summit Meeting," press release, September 24, 2021, https://www.mofa.go.jp/a_o/ocn/au/page4e_001177.html; and "Japan Australia Summit Meeting," Ministry of Foreign Affairs of Japan, press release, June 13, 2021, https://www.mofa.go.jp/a_o/ocn/au/page1e_000327.html.

290 "Fact Sheet: 2020 U.S.-Taiwan Consultations on Democratic Governance in the Indo-Pacific Region and Beyond," American Institute in Taiwan, October 28, 2020, https://www.ait.org.tw/fact-sheet-2020-us-taiwan-consultations-on-democratic-governance-in-indo-pacific/.

291 Prime Minister of Australia, "Joint Statement of the Governments of Australia, Japan and the United States," press release, November 17, 2018, https://www.pm.gov.au/media/joint-statement-governments-australia-japan-and-united-states.

292 Jagannath Panda, "Shinzo Abe's infrastructure diplomacy," *Asia Times*, July 31, 2020, https://asiatimes.com/2020/07/shinzo-abes-infrastructure-diplomacy/; and Patrick W. Quirk, David O. Shullman, and Johanna Kao, "Democracy First: How the U.S. Can Prevail in the Political Systems Competition with the CCP," Brookings Institute, September 2020, https://www.brookings.edu/wp-content/uploads/2020/09/FP_20200914_democracy_assistance_quirk_shullman_kao.pdf.

293 U.S. International Development Finance Corporation, "The Launch of Multi-Stakeholder Blue Dot Network," press release, November 4, 2019, https://www.dfc.gov/media/opic-press-releases/launch-multi-stakeholder-blue-dot-network.

294 Rajeswari Pillai Rajagopalan, "Australia-Japan-India Trilateral Sets Sights on Supply Chain Resilience," *The Diplomat*, October 2, 2020, https://thediplomat.com/2020/10/australia-japan-india-trilateral-sets-sights-on-supply-chain-resilience.

295 Priya Chacko and Jeffrey Wilson, *Australia, Japan and India: A trilateral coalition in the Indo-Pacific?* (Perth: Perth USAsia Centre, September 2020), https://perthusasia.edu.au/getattachment/Our-Work/Australia,-Japan-and-India-A-trilateral-coalition/PU-175-AJI-Book-WEB(2).pdf.aspx?lang=en-AU.

296 Ryo Sahashi, Alison Szalwinski, John S. Park, and Roy D. Kamphausen, *The Case for U.S.-ROK-Japan Trilateralism: Strengths and Limitations* (Washington, DC: National Bureau of Asian Research, February 2018), https://www.nbr.org/publication/the-case-for-u-s-rok-japan-trilateralism-strengths-and-limitations/.

297 "Joint Statement on U.S.-Japan-ROK Women's Empowerment Trilateral Forum," U.S. Embassy and Consulate in the Republic of Korea.

298 Ministry of Foreign Affairs Republic of Korea, "'The 2nd ROK-US-Japan omen's Empowerment Trilateral Conference' to Take Place," press release, October 19, 2020, https://www.mofa.go.kr/eng/brd/m_5676/view.do?seq=321285&srchFr=&srchTo=&srchWord=Forum&srchTp=&multi_itm_seq=0&itm_seq_1=0&itm_seq_2=0&company_cd=&company_nm=&page=44&titleNm=.

299 Ministry of Foreign Affairs of Japan, "23rd Japan-ASEAN Summit Meeting," press release, November 12, 2020, https://www.mofa.go.jp/a_o/rp/page3e_001075.html.

300 Ministry of Foreign Affairs of Japan, *Japan's Cooperation Projects on AOIP as of Nov. 2020: Example of the projects* (Tokyo: November 2020), https://www.mofa.go.jp/files/100115874.pdf.

301 "[FACT SHEET] United States-ASEAN Strategic Partnership," U.S. Mission to ASEAN, September 9, 2020, https://asean.usmission.gov/fact-sheet-united-states-asean-strategic-partnership/.

302 Ibid.

303 "The Plan of Action to Implement the ASEAN-United States Strategic Partnership (2021-2025)," ASEAN, September 10, 2020, https://asean.org/speechandstatement/plan-of-action-to-implement-the-asean-united-states-strategic-partnership-2021-2025/.

304 Ibid.

305 Office of the Spokesperson, U.S. Department of State, "The United States and ASEAN: Strategic Partners for the Indo-Pacific," press release, August 4, 2021, https://www.state.gov/the-united-states-and-asean-strategic-partners-for-the-indo-pacific/.

306 "Japan, U.S., India, Australia call for return of democracy in Myanmar," Reuters, February 18, 2021, https://www.reuters.com/article/us-usa-blinken-quad-myanmar/japan-u-s-india-australia-call-for-return-of-democracy-in-myanmar-idUSKBN2AI20K.

307 "Quad Leaders' Joint Statement: 'The Spirit of the Quad'," The White House, Statements and Releases, March 12, 2021, https://www.whitehouse.gov/briefing-room/statements-releases/2021/03/12/quad-leaders-joint-statement-the-spirit-of-the-quad/.

308 "Joint Statement from Quad Leaders," The White House, Statements and Releases, September 24, 2021, https://www.whitehouse.gov/briefing-room/statements-releases/2021/09/24/joint-statement-from-quad-leaders/.

309 Niranjan Sahoo and Maiko Ichihara, "The Quad Can End the Crisis in Myanmar," *Foreign Policy*, March 19, 2021, https://foreignpolicy.com/2021/03/19/quad-myanmar-crisis-protests-india-japan-tatmadaw/. See also Quad joint statements from March 2021 and September 2021.

310 Patrick Gerard Buchan and Benjamin Rimland, "Defining the Diamond: The Past, Present, and Future of the Quadrilateral Security Dialogue," CSIS, *CSIS Brief*, March 16, 2020, https://www.csis.org/analysis/defining-diamond-past-present-and-future-quadrilateral-security-dialogue.

311 Dian Septiari, "Concern for democracy overshadows international Bali forum," *Jakarta Post*, December 4, 2019, https://www.thejakartapost.com/news/2019/12/04/concern-for-democracy-to-overshadow-international-bali-forum.html.

312 "Documents of BDF 13th 2020," Bali Democracy Forum, n.d., https://bdf.kemlu.go.id/publication/docs-of-bdf-13.

313 National Coordination Team of South-South Cooperation, *Annual Report of Indonesia's South-South and Triangular Cooperation (SSTC) 2016* (Jakarta: Government of Indonesia and JICA, 2017), https://openjicareport.jica.go.jp/pdf/12315719.pdf.

314 Ibid.

315 "Partnership Initiative for SSTC," Indonesia UNDP, accessed July 28, 2021, https://www.id.undp.org/content/indonesia/en/home/projects/South-south-and-triangular-cooperation.html.

316 "Chairman's Statement of the 27th Regional Forum," ASEAN, September 12, 2020, https://asean.org/chairmans-statement-of-the-27th-asean-regional-forum/.

317 "ASEAN Plus Three Cooperation Work Plan (2018-2022)," ASEAN, August 7, 2017, https://asean.org/asean-plus-three-cooperation-work-plan-2018-2022/.

318 Daniel F. Runde and Shannon McKeown, *The Asian Development Bank: A Strategic Asset for the United States* (Washington, DC: CSIS, December 18, 2019), https://www.csis.org/analysis/asian-development-bank-strategic-asset-united-states.

319 Ibid.

320 Asian Development Bank (ADB), *Strategy 2030* (Manila: July 2018), https://www.adb.org/sites/default/files/institutional-document/435391/strategy-2030-main-document.pdf.

321 APEC, "Senior Officials Expedite Regional Response to COVID-19, Push Recovery Process," press release, March 2021, https://www.apec.org/Press/News-Releases/2021/0312_SOM1.

322 APEC Policy Support Unit, *Renewed APEC Agenda for Structural Reform (RAASR) - Final Review Report* (Singapore: APEC, August 2020), https://www.apec.org/Publications/2020/10/Renewed-APEC-Agenda-for-Structural-Reform-RAASR---Final-Review-Report.

323 "Anti-Corruption and Transparency," APEC, February 2021, https://www.apec.org/Groups/SOM-Steering-Committee-on-Economic-and-Technical-Cooperation/Working-Groups/Anti-Corruption-and-Transparency.

324 "Policy Partnership on Women and the Economy," APEC, August 2019, https://www.apec.org/groups/som-steering-committee-on-economic-and-technical-cooperation/working-groups/policy-partnership-on-women-and-the-economy.

325 "A Guide to IORA," IORA, April 2020, https://www.iora.int/en.

326 Sato, "Japan's Approach to Global Democracy Support"; Hall, "Not Promoting, Not Exporting"; and "Multilateral aid effectiveness," Government of Australia, DFAT, n.d., https://www.dfat.gov.au/aid/who-we-work-with/multilateral-organisations/Pages/multilateral-organisations.

327 "Status of Contributions in US Dollars," United Nations Democracy Fund, n.d., https://www.un.org/democracyfund/sites/www.un.org.democracyfund/files/contributions_undef_2005-20211104.pdf.

328 "United Nations: UNDP and UNICEF," Australian Government, DFAT, n.d., https://www.dfat.gov.au/development/who-we-work-with/multilateral-organisations/Pages/united-nations-unicef.

329 Ibid.

330 "Partnerships for Recovery and gender equality," Government of Australia.

331 "Donor Details," United Nations Office on Drugs and Crime, n.d., https://www.unodc.org/unodc/en/donors/grants-opendata.html.

332 "UN Women in India," UN Women: Asia and the Pacific, 2013, https://asiapacific.unwomen.org/en/digital-library/publications/2012/5/un-women-in-india.

333 Hall, "Not Promoting, Not Exporting."

334 Ibid.

335 Development Aid, "Indonesia launches an International Development Aid Fund. A look back at Indonesia's aid history," press release, December 9, 2019, https://www.developmentaid.org/#!/news-stream/post/55554/indonesia-launches-an-international-development-aid-fund-a-look-back-at-indonesias-aid-history.

336 Sato, "Japan's Approach to Global Democracy Support."

337 "Top government partners," UN Women, n.d., https://www.unwomen.org/en/partnerships/donor-countries/top-donors.

338 Geiger, *Japan's Support for Democracy-Related Issues*.

339 Ibid.

340   KOICA Strategy and Policy Planning for Development Programs Team, *Mid-to-long term implementation plans.*

341   Atkinson, "Comparing Taiwan's foreign aid to Japan, South Korea and DAC."

342   Ibid.

343   "G7 Summit Discusses Inequalities, Global Environmental Challenges," International Institute for Sustainable Development, August 29, 2019, https://sdg.iisd.org/news/g7-summit-discusses-inequalities-global-environmental-challenges/.

344   "'Unanimous' G7 support for RSF's Information and Democracy Initiative," Reporters without Borders, August 26, 2019, https://rsf.org/en/news/unanimous-g7-support-rsfs-information-and-democracy-initiative.

345   "G7 Statement on Hong Kong Electoral Changes," U.S. Department of State, March 12, 2021, https://www.state.gov/g7-statement-on-hong-kong-electoral-changes/.

346   The White House, "Cabbis Bay G7 Summit Communiqué," Statements and Releases, June 13, 2021, https://www.whitehouse.gov/briefing-room/statements-releases/2021/06/13/carbis-bay-g7-summit-communique/.

347   Ibid.

348   Ibid.

349   "G7 and Guest Countries: 2021 Open Societies Statement," Ministry of External Affairs, Government of India, June 13, 2021, https://www.mea.gov.in/bilateral-documents.htm?dtl/33910/G7+and+Guest+Countries+2021+Open+Socities+Statement.

350   Patrick Wintour, "Boris Johnson to visit India in January in bid to transform G7," *The Guardian*, December 5, 2020, https://www.theguardian.com/world/2020/dec/15/boris-johnson-to-visit-india-in-january-in-bid-to-transform-g7.

www.ingramcontent.com/pod-product-compliance
Lightning Source LLC
Chambersburg PA
CBHW080414300426
44113CB00015B/2515